AGES 5–7

p

Helping your child

- Remember that the activities in this book should be enjoyed by your child.

- Try to find a quiet place to work.

- Your child does not need to complete each page all at once. Always stop before your child grows tired, and come back to the same page another time.

- It is important to work through the pages in the right order because the activities become progressively more difficult.

- Always give your child lots of encouragement and praise.

- Remember that the gold stars are a reward for effort as well as achievement.

Written by Shaynie Morris
Illustrations by Lynda Murray, Dorian Spencer Davies (Beehive Illustrations) and Jim Peacock
Design by Thelma-Jane Robb and Gary Knight

This is a Parragon Publishing book
This edition published in 2003

Parragon Publishing
Queen Street House
4 Queen Street
Bath BA1 1HE, UK

ISBN 1-40541-718-8
Printed in Malaysia

Contents

This book belongs to

Writing

The activities in this section help children to practice writing individual letters and words, to organize words into lists, and to write labels. The activities encourage the use of punctuation and provide opportunities for creative writing.

⭐ Trace over the dotted letters. Then practice writing some on your own. Remember to start at the red dot each time.

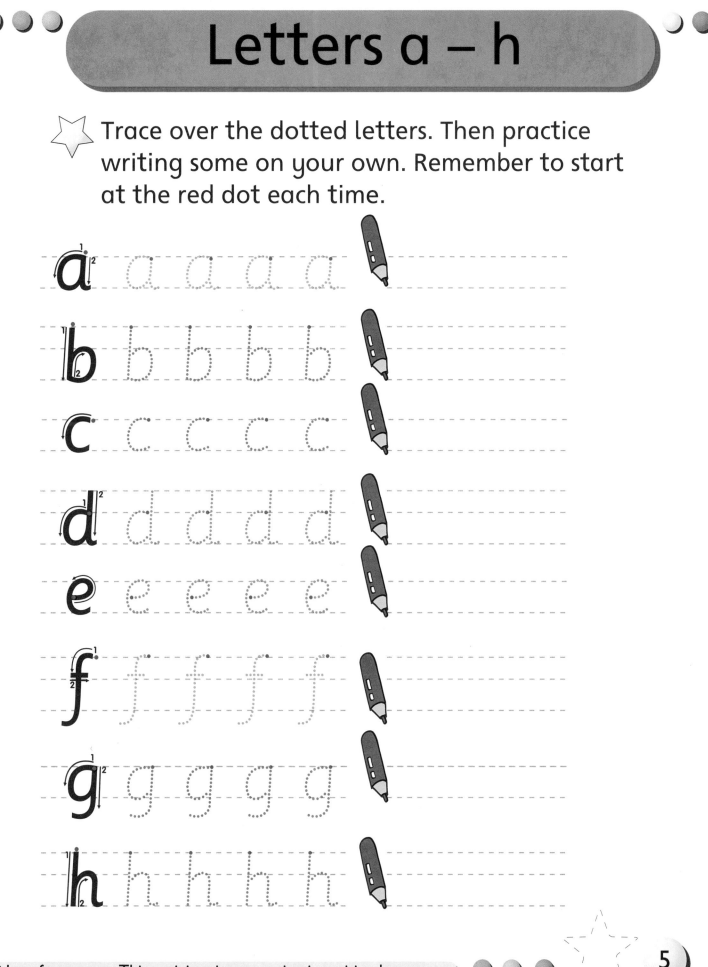

Note for parent: This activity gives practice in writing letters.

5

Letters i – z

⭐ Trace over the dotted letters. Then practice writing some on your own. Remember to start at the red dot each time.

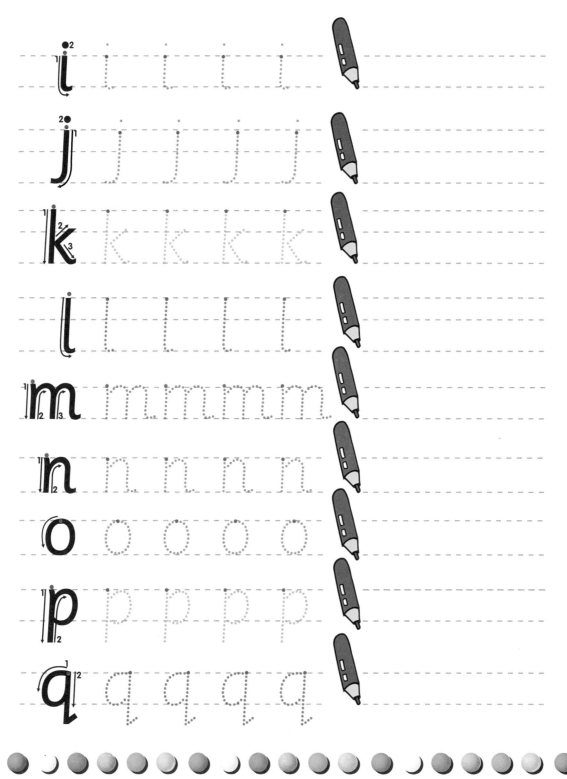

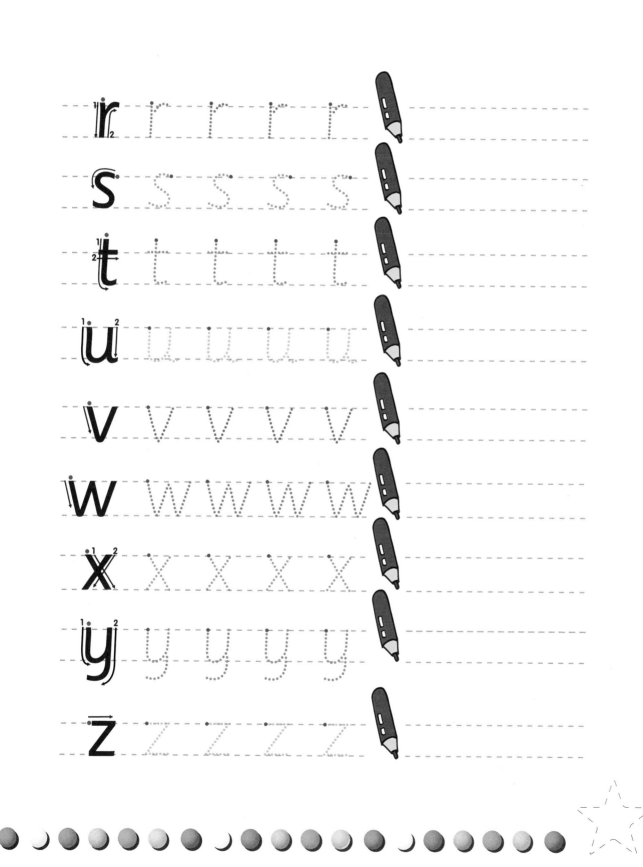

r r r r r r

s s s s s

t t t t t

u u u u u

v v v v v

w w w w w

x x x x x

y y y y y

z z z z z

Space search

Trace over the dotted words below.
Find and circle the words in the word search.
The first one has been done for you.

sun   rocket   planet
meteor   galaxy   star
moon   comet   crater

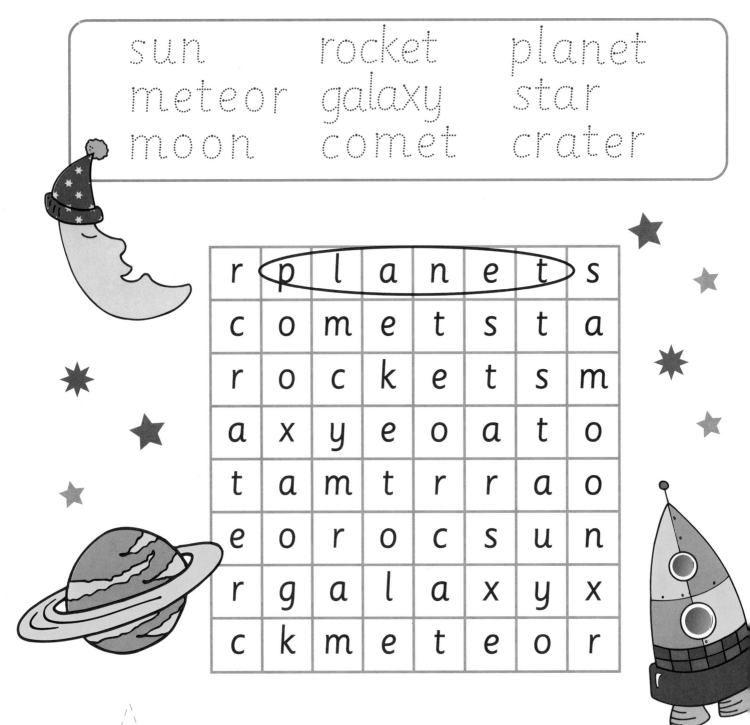

r	p	l	a	n	e	t	s
c	o	m	e	t	s	t	a
r	o	c	k	e	t	s	m
a	x	y	e	o	a	t	o
t	a	m	t	r	r	a	o
e	o	r	o	c	s	u	n
r	g	a	l	a	x	y	x
c	k	m	e	t	e	o	r

⭐ Trace over the dotted words. Then read what each person is saying.

I am *five* years old.

My *cat* is called Fred.

I love *pizza*.

Join the letters

☆ Draw a line to join each small letter to the correct capital letter. The first one has been done for you.

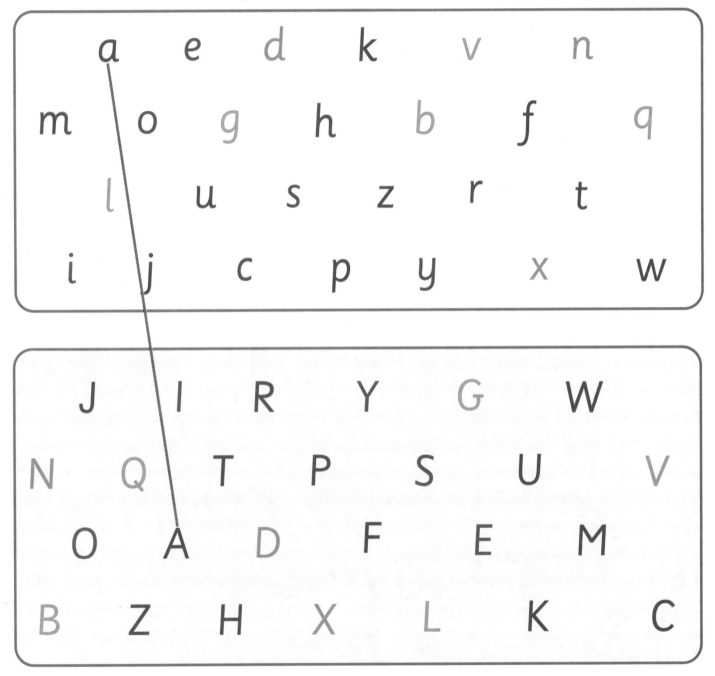

Capital or small?

Look at the pictures. Do the words begin with a small letter or a capital letter? Write your answers in the boxes.

☐ luffy

F or f

☐ ooks

B or b

☐ ally

S or s

☐ avid

D or d

☐ able

T or t

☐ at

H or h

Which book?

Julie wants to find out about the subjects in the pictures below. Which books does she need? Can you find the first letter of each word on the shelf? Write the book numbers in the boxes.

| 1 a-b | 2 c-d | 3 e-f | 4 g-h | 5 i-j | 6 k-l | 7 m-n | 8 o-p | 9 q-r | 10 s-t | 11 u-v | 12 w-x | 13 y-z |

horses [4]

dinosaurs [ ]

trains [ ]

insects [ ]

snow [ ]

queens [ ]

alligators [ ]

Note for parent: This activity provides practice in putting words into alphabetical order.

Address book

Bob's address book is missing some names. The names are written on the left of this page. Write them in for him. Be sure they are in alphabetical order. The first one has been done.

Fred

David

Billy

Eve

Chris

Alison
41 Church Street

Billy
24 Spring Road

_____
7 Bridge Street

_____
32 Main Street

_____
15 Pretty Drive

_____
2 Forest Lane

Street index

Look up these street names in the index on the facing page. Write the page numbers in the boxes.

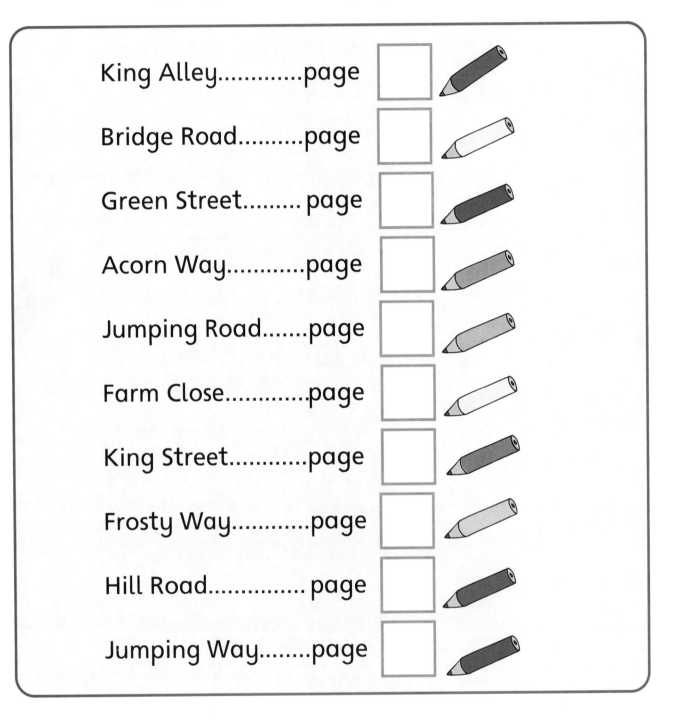

King Alley............page ☐

Bridge Road.........page ☐

Green Street......... page ☐

Acorn Way...........page ☐

Jumping Road.......page ☐

Farm Close...........page ☐

King Street...........page ☐

Frosty Way...........page ☐

Hill Road.............. page ☐

Jumping Way........page ☐

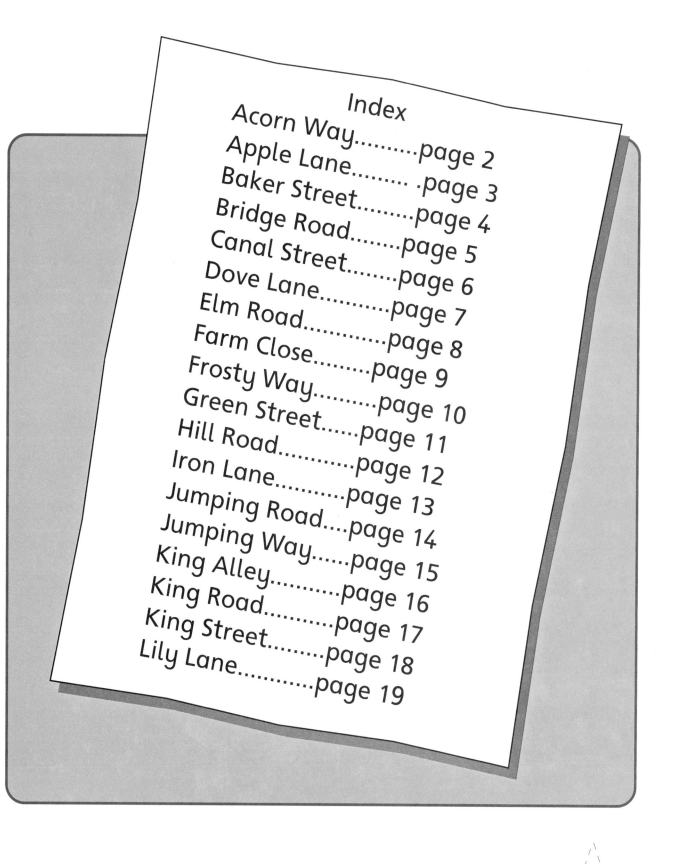

Index

Say the names

⭐ Say the name of each animal. Write another word that begins with the same sound.

dog
d _____

bear
b _____

horse
h _____

tiger
t _____

cow
c _____

penguin
p _____

snake
s _____

monkey
m _____

Note for parent: This activity gives practice in identifying beginning sounds.

Finish the sentences

Finish the sentences with a word that begins with the same letter. Write your answers on the lines. Use the words at the bottom to help you.

Sam sang silly _____ .

Bob blew big _____ .

Laura loves little _____ .

Tim tripped two _____ .

Wendy watches wild _____ .

Meg made more _____ .

songs	macaroni
waves	times
ladybugs	bubbles

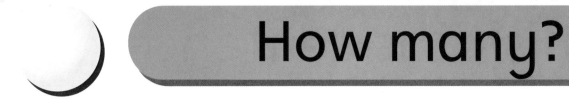

How many things can you see that begin with the letter S? Write them on the lines.

How many things can you see that begin with the letter p? Write them on the lines.

How many things can you see that begin with the letter *f*? Write them on the lines.

_____

_____

How many things can you see that begin with the letter *b*? Write them on the lines.

_____

_____

Rhyming words

Say aloud each word below. Draw a line from each word on the left to the color that rhymes.

clown

green

queen

red

bed

brown

sink

gray

kite

white

hay

pink

Note for parent: Finding words that rhyme encourages children to listen carefully.

Write a rhyme

Write a rhyme

⭐ Say the name of each object. Write a word that rhymes with each one.

train

dog

mop

flag

cake

tree

Circus words

Read the words in the blue boxes. Can you find something in the picture that rhymes with each one? Use the words in the box below to help you. Write your answers on the lines.

ball man clown
hat shoe

blue

_____

mat

_____

tall

_____

can

frown

Word search

Look carefully at the pictures. Find the name of each animal in the word search. Write an animal's name next to each picture. The first one has been done for you.

snake

h	o	h	o	r	s	e	t
p	e	n	g	u	i	n	i
e	b	p	e	w	d	o	g
n	g	i	r	a	f	f	e
g	u	g	o	b	e	a	r
z	i	c	s	h	s	r	s
e	m	o	n	k	e	y	e
b	l	w	a	b	a	e	r
r	z	o	k	r	l	t	g
a	s	w	e	s	h	c	f

snake   horse
pig   zebra
monkey   penguin
tiger   cow

Note for parent: This activity gives children practice in writing and labeling objects.

Picture puzzle

Look at the picture clues. Use the names of the pictures to complete the word grid.

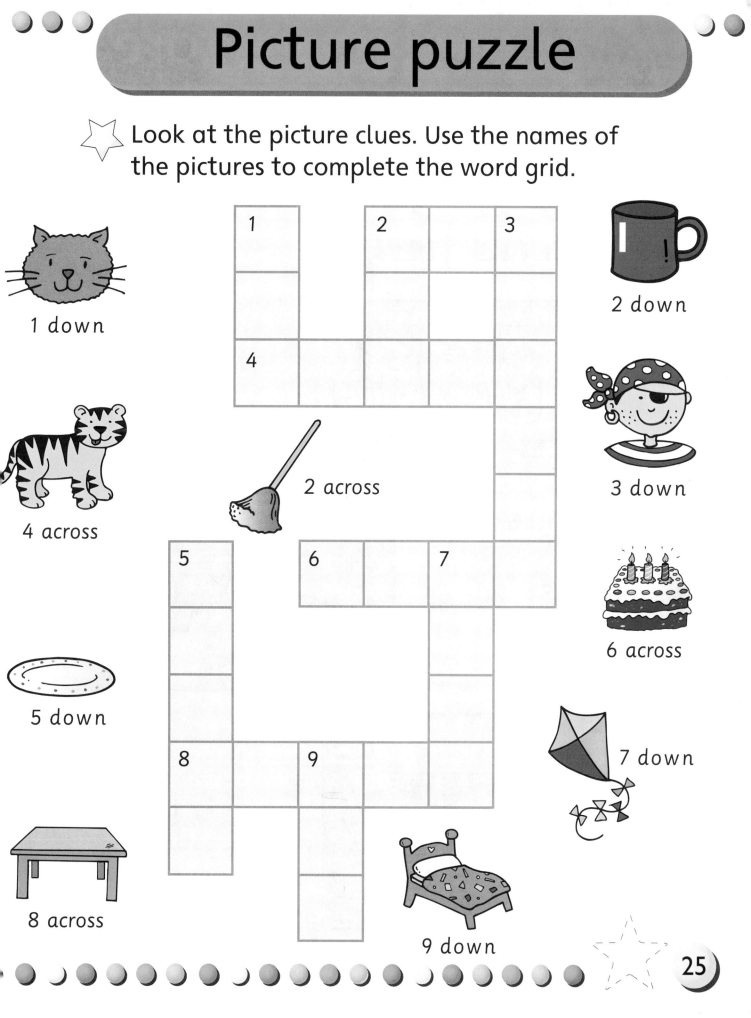

1 down

2 down

4 across

3 down

2 across

5 down

6 across

5

6

7

7 down

8 across

8

9

9 down

⭐ Write the correct labels in the signs to show the departments in the store. Use the words in the boxes to help you.

Bedding

Shoes

Clothes

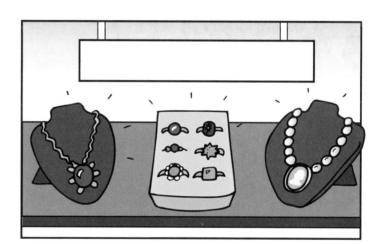

Kitchen goods

Perfumes

Jewellery

Shopping list

⭐ The pictures show foods you need to buy at the supermarket. Write the name of each food on the list. The first one has been done for you.

bread

bananas

jelly

cookies

milk

potatoes

shopping list

bread
_____
_____
_____
_____
_____
_____
_____
_____

pie

peas

cheese

apples

Picnic list

⭐ The teddy bears are going on a picnic. Write a list of the things they would like to eat. Use the pictures around the page to help you.

juice

apples

cakes

sandwiches

pizza

⭐ Write a list of the other things they will need.

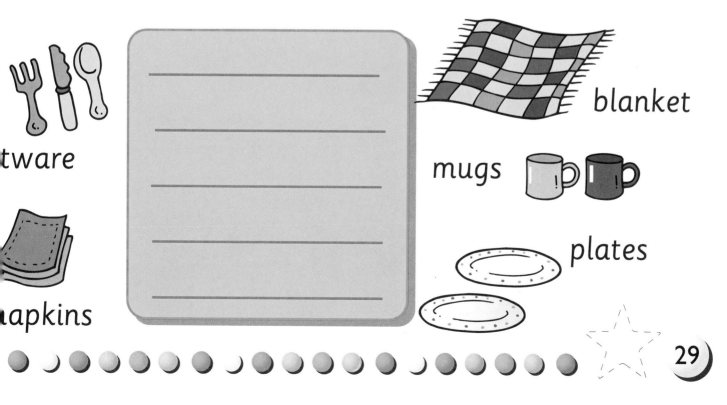

blanket

tware

mugs

plates

apkins

Party time!

It's time to plan a party. Write a list of four people you will invite.

Jack

Sue

Mark

Jane

Ben

Laura

Anne

Andrew

_____

_____

_____

_____

Now write a list of four things you will need.

food

music

balloons

drinks

hats

games

_____

_____

_____

_____

What's in your room?

⭐ Write a list of some of the things in your bedroom.

My things

_____

_____

_____

_____

_____

How many of each do you have?

books ☐

toys ☐

pillows ☐

socks ☐

t-shirts ☐

shoes ☐

Punctuation

You put a period at the end of a sentence. You put a question mark at the end of a sentence that asks a question. You put an exclamation mark at the end of a sentence with a special meaning.

Write the correct punctuation at the end of each sentence below. The first one has been done for you.

Does it need a...

● period   **?** question mark   **!** exclamation mark

Are you going swimming **?**

That's great ☐

It's my birthday ☐

What time is it ☐

I am six years old ☐

Note for parent: This activity gives practice in punctuation.

Recipes

The recipes are in a muddle! Write in commas to separate the ingredients in the lists. The first one has been done for you.

1 eggs, bacon, peppers, onions

2 flour sugar water milk butter

3 pasta tomatoes onions garlic

4 chicken carrots celery herbs

5 dough tomato sauce cheese mushrooms

6 bread lettuce tomatoes cheese

List the foods

⭐ Look at the foods in each row. Write the names of the foods on the lines. Use commas in between the words.

milk   butter   bread

French stick   cheese   carrots

eggs   hamburger   fries

Code words

Nick and Anna are playing hide-and-seek.
Use the code to find out where Anna is hiding.

1	=	n	5	=	h	9	=	t
2	=	i	6	=	d	10	=	e
3	=	a	7	=	g	11	=	b
4	=	s	8	=	u	12	=	r

?

```
___ ___ ___      ___ ___
 4   5  10        2   4

___ ___ ___ ___ ___ ___
 5   2   6   2   1   7

    ___ ___ ___ ___ ___
     8   1   6  10  12

    ___ ___ ___   ___ ___ ___
     9   5  10    11  10   6
```

Note for parent: This activity provides practice in writing letters.

Read the recipe

⭐ Read the recipe. Then answer the questions.

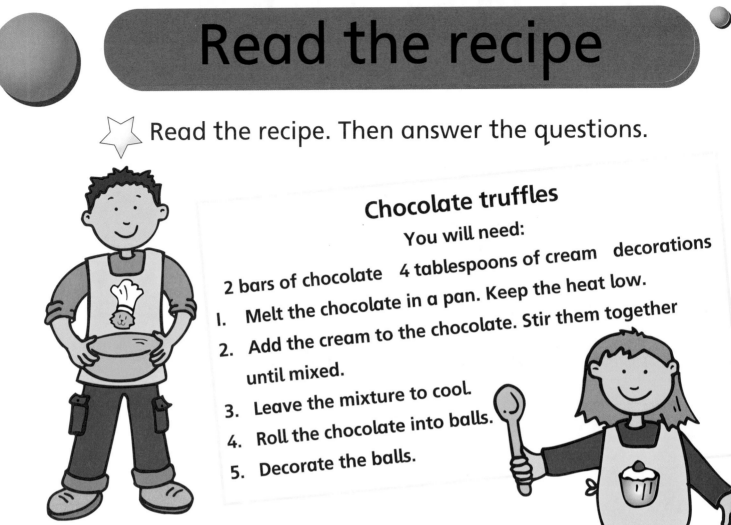

Chocolate truffles
You will need:

2 bars of chocolate   4 tablespoons of cream   decorations

1. Melt the chocolate in a pan. Keep the heat low.
2. Add the cream to the chocolate. Stir them together until mixed.
3. Leave the mixture to cool.
4. Roll the chocolate into balls.
5. Decorate the balls.

1. How many tablespoons of cream do you need?   _____

2. How many bars of chocolate do you need?   _____

3. What else do you need?   _____

4. When do you add the cream?   _____

5. Does the mixture have to cool?   _____

Note for parent: This activity encourages children to understand the importance of sequence and of following instructions.

Help the builders

Read the building plans. Follow the instructions to show the builders what to build.

1. Draw a rectangle at the bottom of the paper. The shortest sides of the rectangle should be on the right and left.
2. Draw 2 squares side-by-side on top of the rectangle. They should both fit evenly on top.
3. Draw a big triangle on top of the squares.
4. Draw a circle in the center of the triangle.
5. Draw 2 squares for windows. Draw a rectangle for the front door.

Go to the zoo

⭐ Read the directions. With a pen or pencil, draw your route on the map.

How to get to the zoo:

1. Drive forward along Happy Street.

2. Take the 2nd on the right into Hilly Lane.

3. Take the 2nd on the right into Park Road.

4. Take the 2nd on the left into Sandy Street. Continue past the school.

5. Turn left at the end and drive over the bridge.

6. The zoo will be on your right.

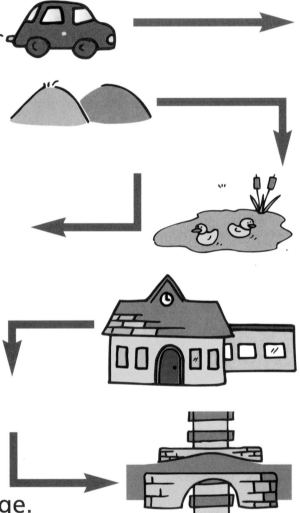

What do you see?

Look at the scene below. What do you see?
Write down the names of 5 things.

1. _____   4. _____

2. _____   5. _____

3. _____

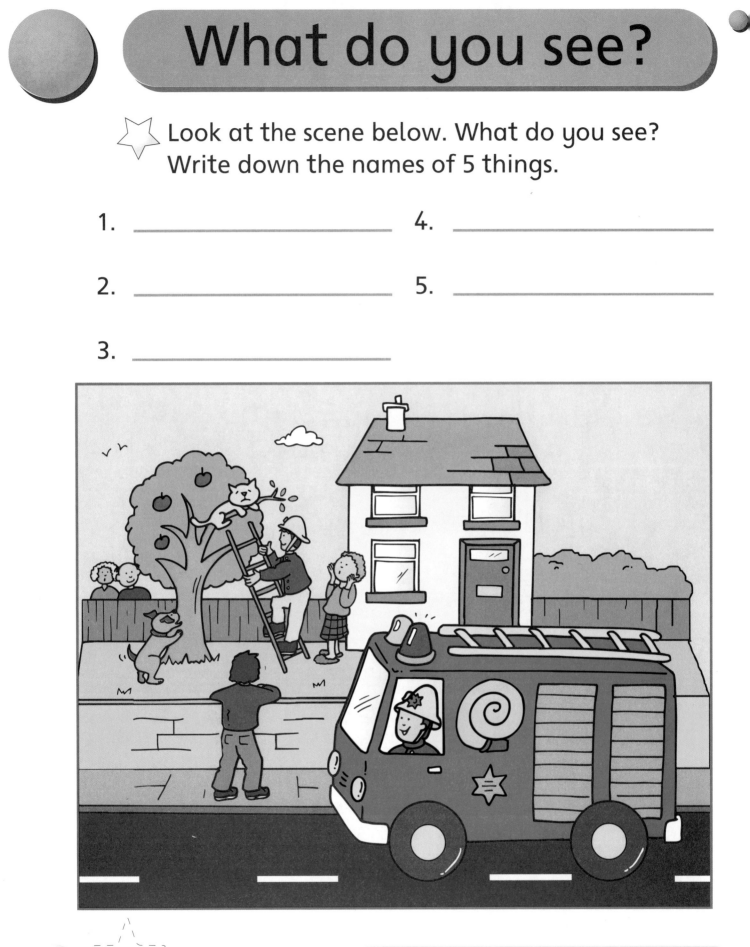

Note for parent: This activity encourages
children to think about and write descriptions.

What am I?

Read the clues. Then draw a line to the correct picture. Write the word by each picture. The first one has been done for you.

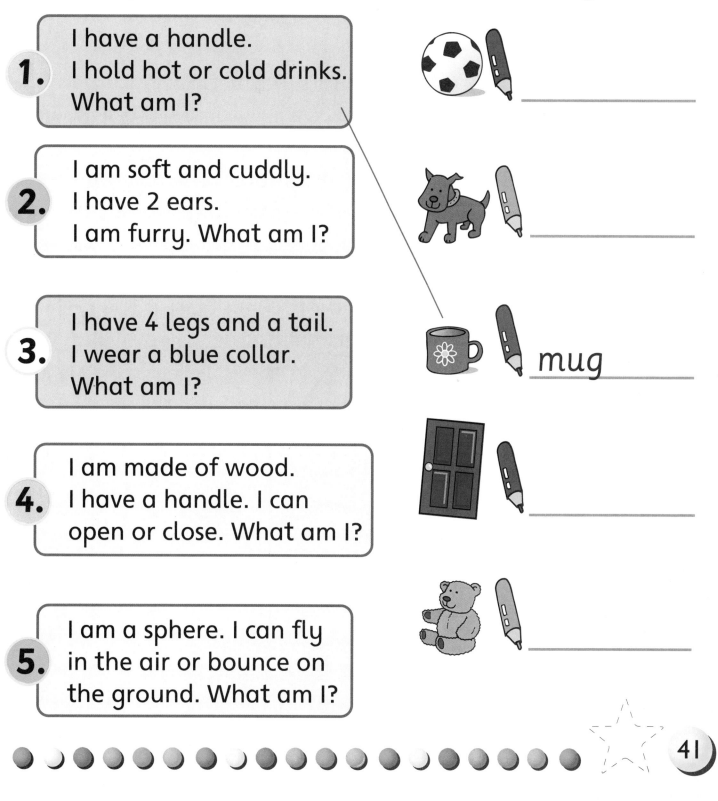

1. I have a handle.
I hold hot or cold drinks.
What am I?

2. I am soft and cuddly.
I have 2 ears.
I am furry. What am I?

3. I have 4 legs and a tail.
I wear a blue collar.
What am I?   mug

4. I am made of wood.
I have a handle. I can
open or close. What am I?

5. I am a sphere. I can fly
in the air or bounce on
the ground. What am I?

Descriptions

An adjective is a describing word. It tells you more about a noun. Write two adjectives that describe each object. Use the words in the box to help you. The first one has been done for you.

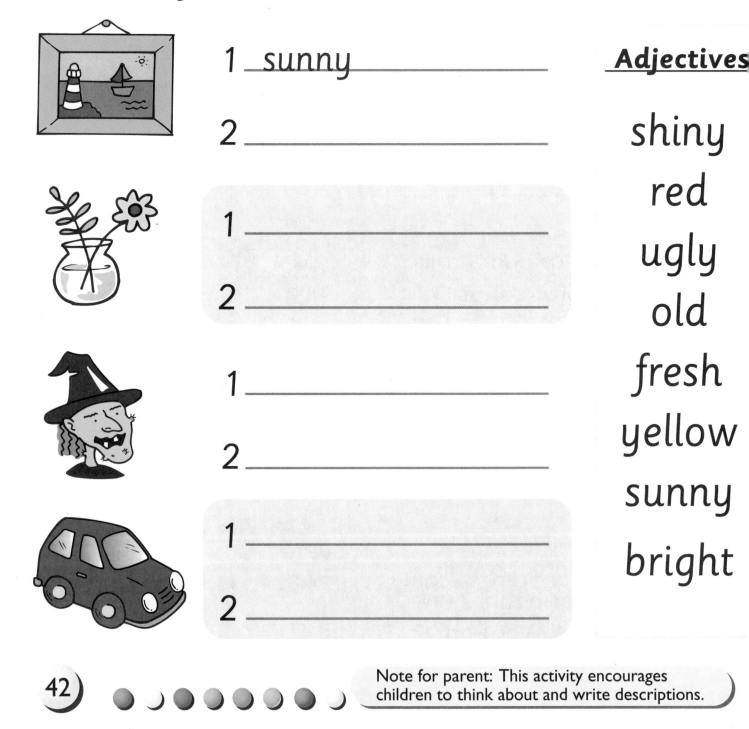

1 _sunny_

2 _____

Adjectives

shiny

red

ugly

old

fresh

yellow

sunny

bright

1 _____

2 _____

1 _____

2 _____

1 _____

2 _____

Note for parent: This activity encourages children to think about and write descriptions.

Look at the two children, Kate and Joe. Answer the questions.

What color is Kate's hair? _____

What color is her dress? _____

What is she wearing
in her hair? _____

Write two adjectives that describe Kate.

1 _____   2 _____

Is Joe's hair straight or curly? _____

Is his shirt striped
or checked? _____

What is he holding? _____

Write two adjectives that describe Joe.

1 _____   2 _____

What's happening?

What do you think is happening in each picture? Write your ideas on the lines. Use the words in the boxes to help you. Remember to write your ideas in complete sentences. The first one has been done for you.

park	friend	town	hungry
tired	cold	school	dinnertime

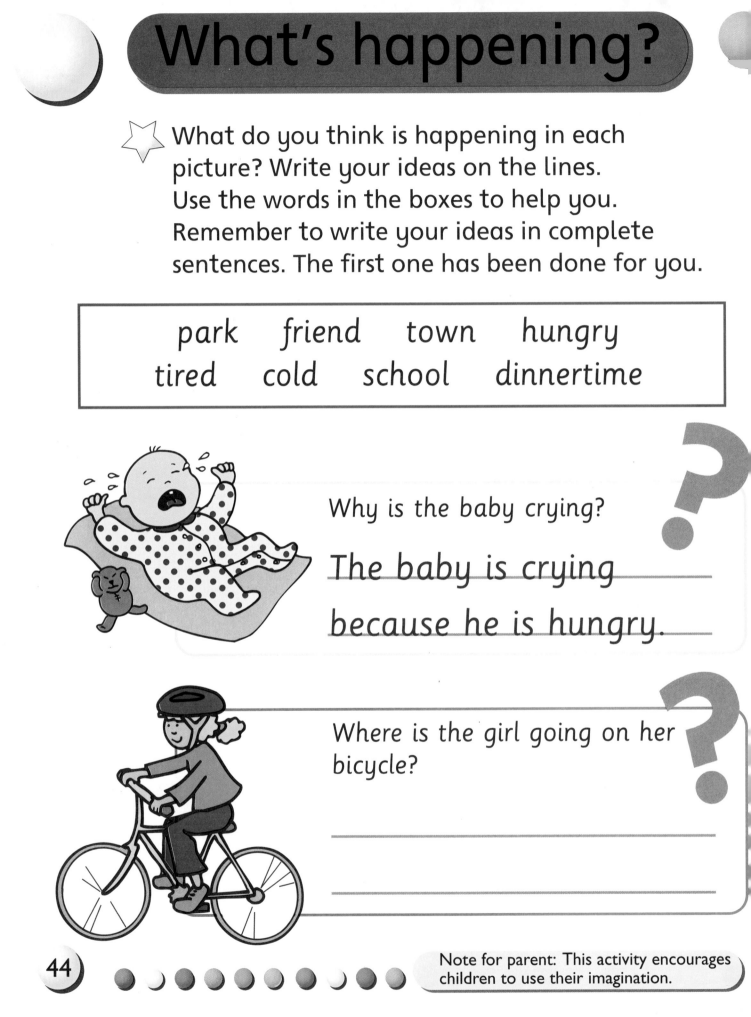

Why is the baby crying?

The baby is crying because he is hungry.

Where is the girl going on her bicycle?

_____

_____

clothes   seaside   country   dog   hall
gift   books   room   chasing   office

Where is Nick going
on holiday?

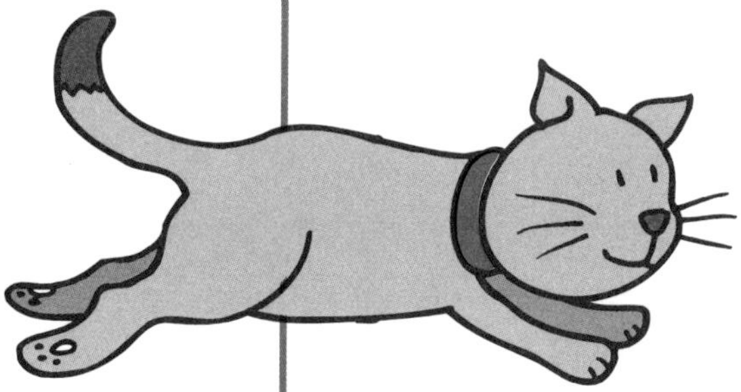

_____

_____

Why is the cat running?

_____

_____

What is behind the door?

_____

_____

What are they saying?

What do you think the characters are saying?
Write your answers in the speech bubbles.
Use the sentences in the boxes to help you.
The first one has been done for you.

I'm a pirate who looks for treasure.
I will make you better when you are ill.

I'm a pirate who looks for treasure.

I'm a scary vampire.
I hope my jokes make you laugh.
I can do magic tricks.

CD cover

The name of this pop group is missing from their CD cover. Write what you think they are called.

Now design your own CD cover. Write the name of the band and draw a picture.

Movie poster

⭐ The words are missing from this movie poster. Write what you think it should say on the lines below.

_____

_____

⭐ Now draw your own movie poster.

Help words

monster

scary

best

movie

noisy

star

Writing cards

Write your own message on each card.

| Thank you | Get well soon |
| Happy birthday | Merry Christmas |

Note for parent: This activity provides practice in creative writing.

Draw a design on the front of this card.
Write a message on it.

Writing a letter

⭐ Read the letter below.

Dear Aunty Sarah,

Hello! How are you? I went swimming yesterday with my friend. We had fun.

Love, Amy

Mrs S. Jones
22 Park Road,
Happyville
W195246-0237

Note for parent: This activity shows children how to write a simple letter.

⭐ Now write your own letter to someone.
Tell them about your day.

Dear _____ ,

_____

_____

_____

_____

_____

from,

Write the name of the person you are writing to here.

What do you want to tell them?

Write your name here.

⭐ Write the name and address on the envelope.

_____

_____

_____

Draw a picture on the stamp.

Read the sign

⭐ Can you read the sign? Use the code to work out what the sign says. Write each letter in the space provided.

1	=	a
2	=	u
3	=	c
4	=	b
5	=	o
6	=	n
7	=	i
8	=	d
9	=	k
10	=	s
11	=	r
12	=	g
13	=	h
14	=	e
15	=	w
16	=	f
17	=	l
18	=	t

```
__ __ __ __ __ __
4  14 15 1  11 14

__ __ __ __ __
8  2  3  9  10

__ __ __ __ __ __ __ __
3  11 5  10 10 7  6  12

__ __ __
18 13 14

__ __ __ __ __
16 7  14 17 8
```

Note for parent: This activity provides practice in solving letter codes.

Crack the code

☆ Can you crack the code to find out where Burglar Ben will rob next?

1 = i	5 = r	9 = o
2 = t	6 = d	10 = a
3 = e	7 = f	11 = g
4 = h	8 = l	12 = y

2 4 3   2 4 1 5 6

7 8 9 9 5   9 7

2 4 3   10 5 2

11 10 8 8 3 5 12

Be the author of your own book! Write your name on the line. Then draw a picture of yourself on the cover.

All About

⭐ Now write some things about yourself.

I am _____ years old. My eyes are _____ and

my hair is _____. My best friend's name

is _____. The people in my

family are: _____

_____

_____

⭐ Draw a picture of your
family here.

My favorite book

⭐ Do you have a favorite book?

What is your favorite book called?

_____

⭐ Draw a picture of the cover.

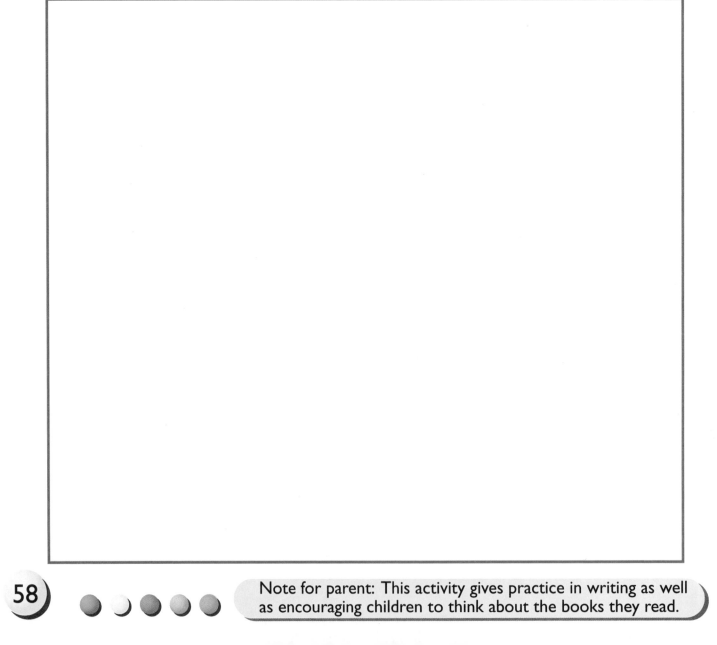

Note for parent: This activity gives practice in writing as well as encouraging children to think about the books they read.

⭐ Write about your favorite book.

What are the characters' names?

_____

_____

What is the book about?

_____

_____

_____

Why do you like it?

_____

_____

Tick the box ✔

I think the book is   ⭐ good   ☐

⭐⭐ very good   ☐

⭐⭐⭐ excellent   ☐

Write a story

⭐ Writing a story can be easy if you have a good idea and you plan it.

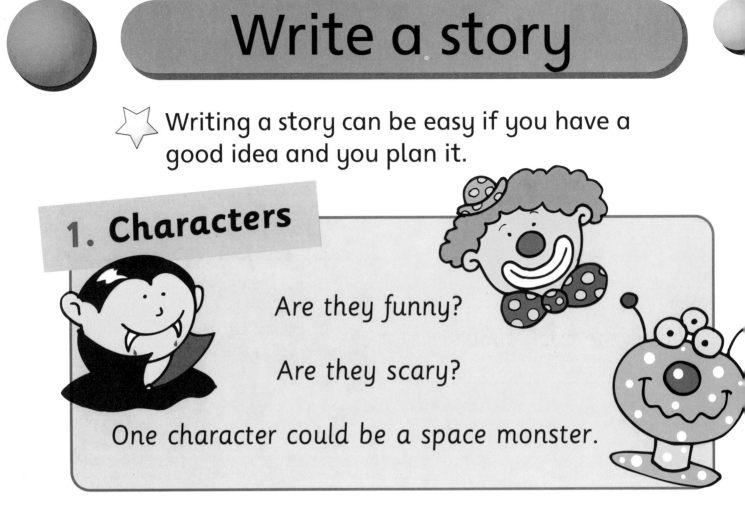

1. Characters

Are they funny?

Are they scary?

One character could be a space monster.

⭐ Think of two characters for your story.
Draw them here. Write their names underneath.

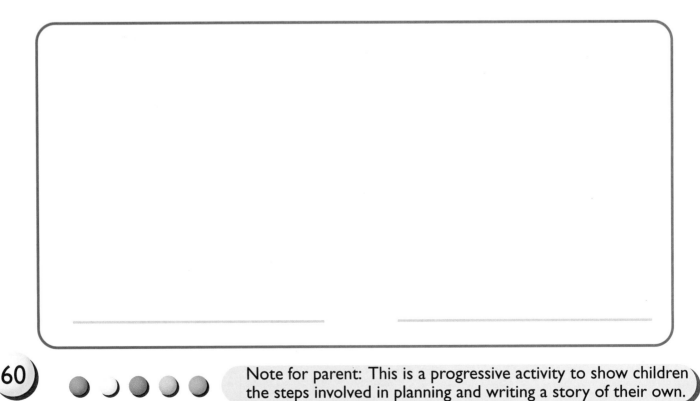

2. Settings

Does your story take place at the circus?

Does it take place in a spooky castle?

Or maybe in space?

⭐ Answer the questions to help you plan your story.

My story takes place in _____ .

The weather is _____ .

Draw a picture for the setting of your story.

Your story

3. Opening

How will your story begin?
Write your idea here.

_____

_____

4. Main event

What is the most important
thing that happens in your story?

_____

_____

5. Ending

How does your story end?

_____

_____

Now it's time to write your story.

Title: _____

This is how my story begins:

This is what happens:

This is how my story ends:

The end

Spelling

The activities in this section will help children to learn and practice basic spelling skills. They encourage children to write out words, identify beginning, middle, and ending sounds, recognize double consonants, and look for spelling patterns.

Animals

Write the first letter of each animal name in the boxes. Use the letters below to help you.

k   t   z   r   g   l

☐ ion

☐ oat

☐ angaroo

☐ urtle

☐ ebra

☐ hinoceros

Note for parent: This activity provides practice in identifying the first letters of words.

Vehicles

Write the first letter of each vehicle in the boxes. Use the letters below to help you.

v   h   c   s   b   r

[ ] oller skates

[ ] an

[ ] ar

[ ] kateboard

[ ] oat

[ ] elicopter

Insects

⭐ Write the first letter of each insect in the boxes. Use the letters below to help you.

s   b   d   a   f   c

☐ nt

☐ pider

☐ ragonfly

☐ utterfly

☐ ly

☐ aterpillar

At the farm

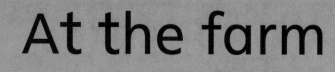

⭐ Look at the picture. What is the last letter of each word label? Write the correct letters on the lines. Use the letters in the box to help you.

tracto___

ha___

hors___

ca___

he___

chic_

Note for parent: This activity provides practice in identifying the last letters of words.

r　y　g　p　n

k　e　w　d　t

shee___

fiel___

co___

Party words

⭐ What is the last letter of each of these words? Write the correct letter on each line. Use the letters below to help you.

e   r   d   n   t

balloo____

cak____

gif____

banne____

car____

70

Note for parent: This activity provides practice in identifying the last letters of words.

Middle vowels

⭐ The letters below are vowels. Without them, you could not make words! Write the correct vowels to complete the words.

a e i o u

w __ n d __ w

l __ m p

r __ g

b __ d

Note for parent: This activity gives practice in
identifying vowels to complete the spellings of words.

71

Which vowels?

⭐ Write the correct vowel to complete the words in the picture below.

a e i o u

tre ___ s

ho ___ se

r ___ ad

c ___ r

p ___ rk

sw ___ ng

New words

Spell each of the words aloud. Then write a new word that begins with each vowel. Write your answers on the lines.

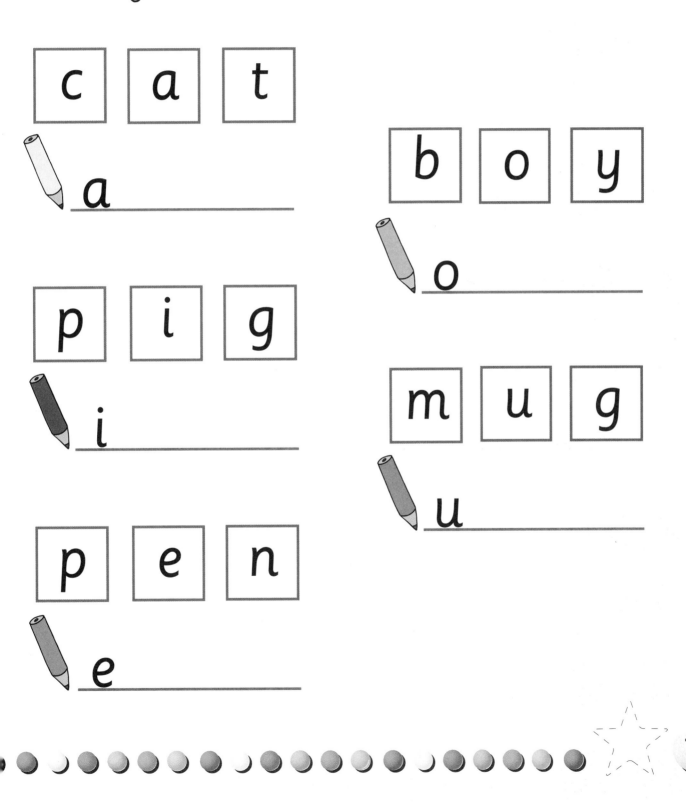

c a t

a _____

b o y

o _____

p i g

i _____

m u g

u _____

p e n

e _____

Missing vowels

Fill in the missing vowels to complete the sentences. Write your answers on the lines.

a	e	i	o	u

The f___t c___t s___t on the m___t.

The fr___g h___pped ___n t___p ___f the m___p.

Th__ wick__d witch fl__w w__st to f__tch a v__st.

The f__rry mo__se ran aro__nd the ho__se.

The p__nk k__te fl__es h__gh __n the sky.

Find the rhymes

⭐ Trace over the dotted letters. Then look at the pictures. Draw a line to join each word to the picture that rhymes with it.

rake

hen

bee

look

man

sing

fog

house

Color the rhymes

Read the words in the box. Look carefully at the picture. Find an object in the kitchen that rhymes with each word. Color the objects.

dish   top   jug

car   jelly

Read the words in the box. Look carefully at the picture. Find an object in the bedroom that rhymes with each word. Color the objects.

hat	wall	mug
stamp	boat	

Yummy cakes

☆ Read each word on the cakes. Draw a line from each cake to the plate with the same beginning sound. The first one has been done for you.

skin

skid

spoon ———————— sp

sk

skip

spin

spot

Note for parent: This activity gives practice in spelling words with two consonants whose sounds blend together at the beginning of a word.

Bees and hives

Read the words beside the bees. Draw a line from each bee to the hive with the same beginning sound.

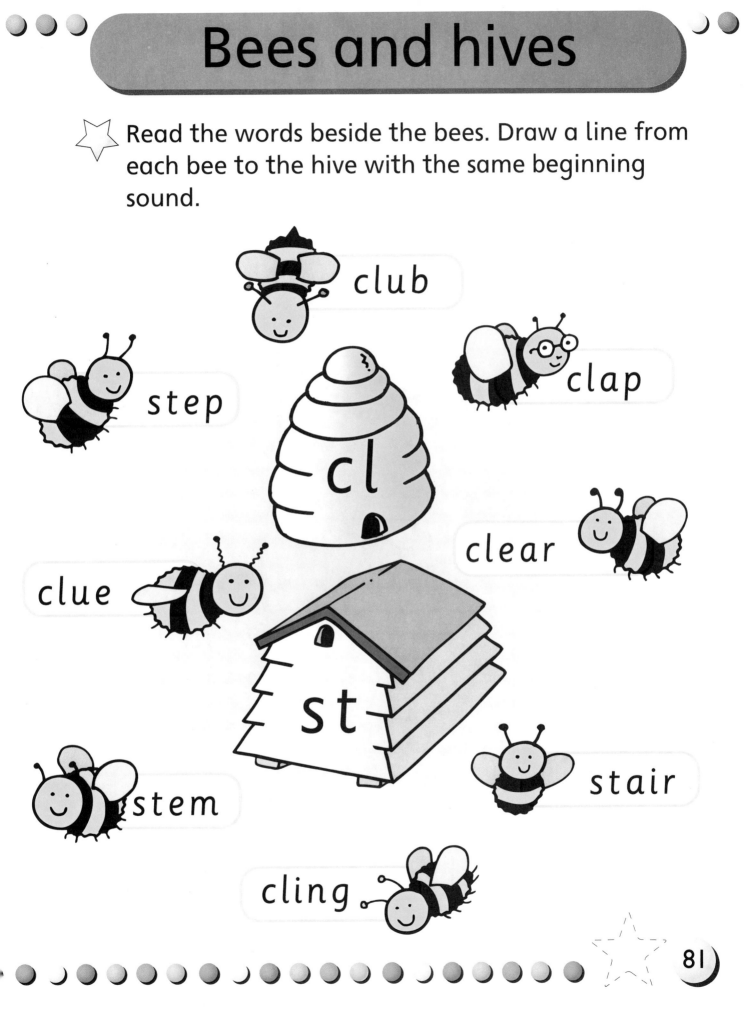

club

step

clap

cl

clue

clear

st

stem

stair

cling

Little mice

Match each mouse hole with a mouse to spell the words below. Draw lines to join them.

clue   stem   drip

spin   flop

Color in blue the spaces with the letters **dr**. Color in yellow the spaces with the letters **fl**.

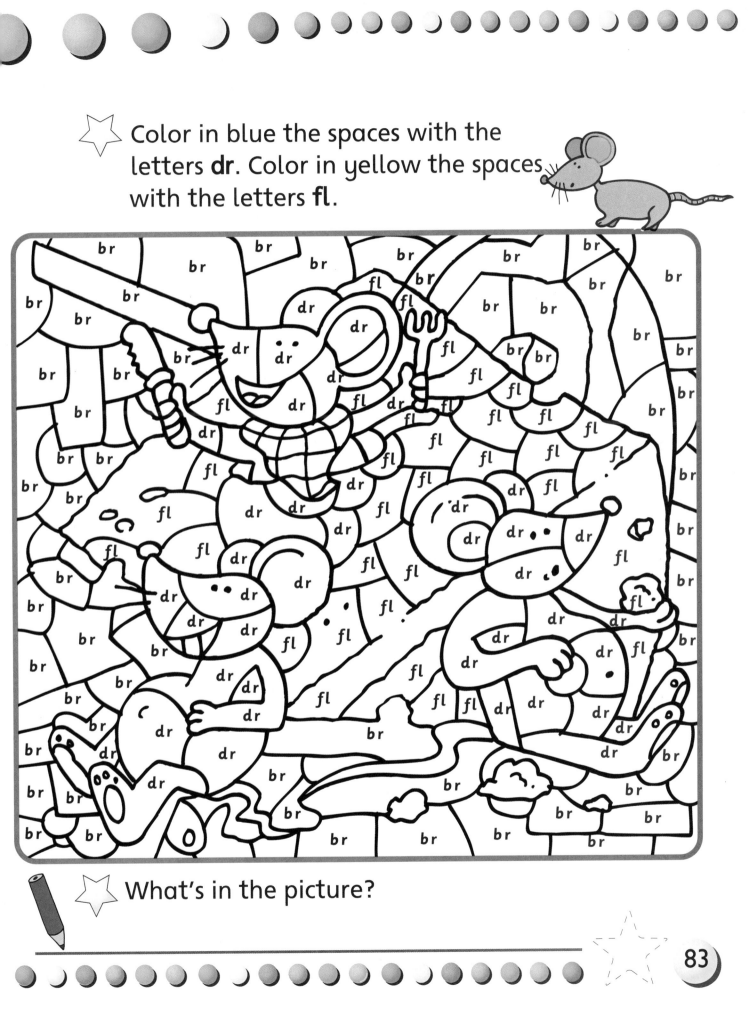

What's in the picture?

_____

Snappy crabs

Match each crab with a rock to spell the words below. Draw lines to join them.

club   drop   snap

slam   spot

sl

ub

cl

op

sn

am

sp

ap

ot

⭐ Color in orange all the spaces with the letters **cl**.

⭐ What's in the picture?

Candy in the jars

Read each word on the candies. Draw a line from each candy to the jar with the same end sound. The first one has been done for you.

hiss

shell

miss

kiss

mess

ball

fuss

less

doll

pull

small

well

s s

l l

Note for parent: This activity provides practice in spelling words that end with double consonants.

Incy wincy spiders

Read each word beside the spiders. Draw a line from each spider to the web with the same end.

nk

ck

wink

drink

pick

tick

sack

lock

pink

blink

rock

sink

clock

sock

Spell the words

Match each child with a skateboard to spell the words in the box. Draw lines to join them. The first one has been done for you.

sock   vest   wand

pink   mess

Color in red all the spaces with the letters **st**.

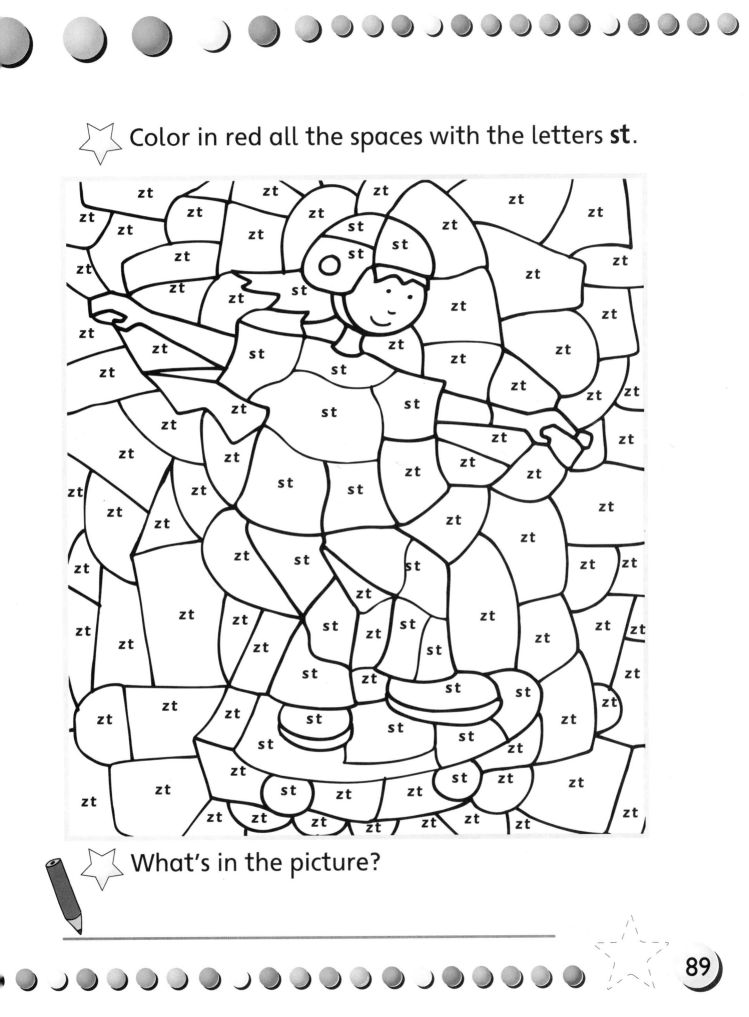

What's in the picture?

Match the eggs

Match the halves of the eggs to spell the words below. Draw lines to join them.

nest	ring	wing
	pull	bend

☆ Color the picture.

☆ What has hatched out of the egg? Write the missing letters in the spaces below.

a d _ n _ sa _ r

Word trail

Look at each of the pictures. Write the names in the spaces to make a word trail.

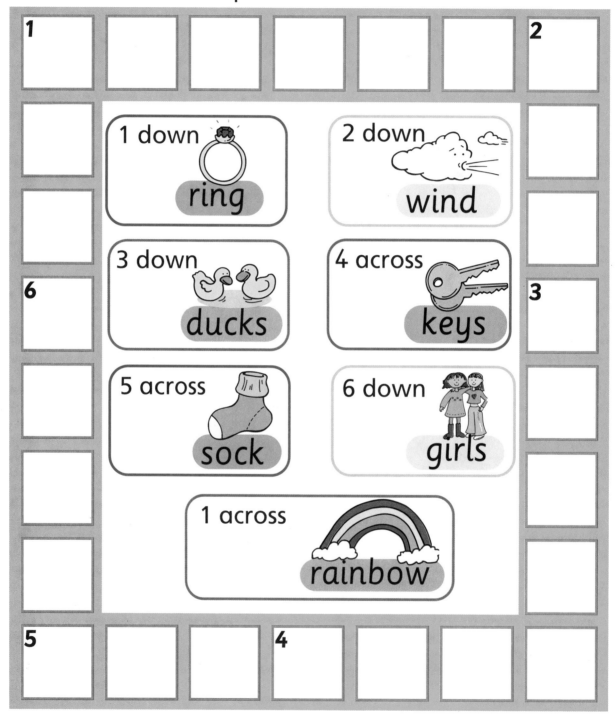

1 down
ring

2 down
wind

3 down
ducks

4 across
keys

5 across
sock

6 down
girls

1 across
rainbow

Note for parent: This activity gives practice in spelling words correctly.

Crossword

Read the clues below. Write the answers in the crossword. Use the pictures to help you.

3 across – Something you write to someone.

2 down – This opens and shuts.

5 down – You hang this on the wall.

4 down – You eat this at a party.

1 across – You make one when it snows.

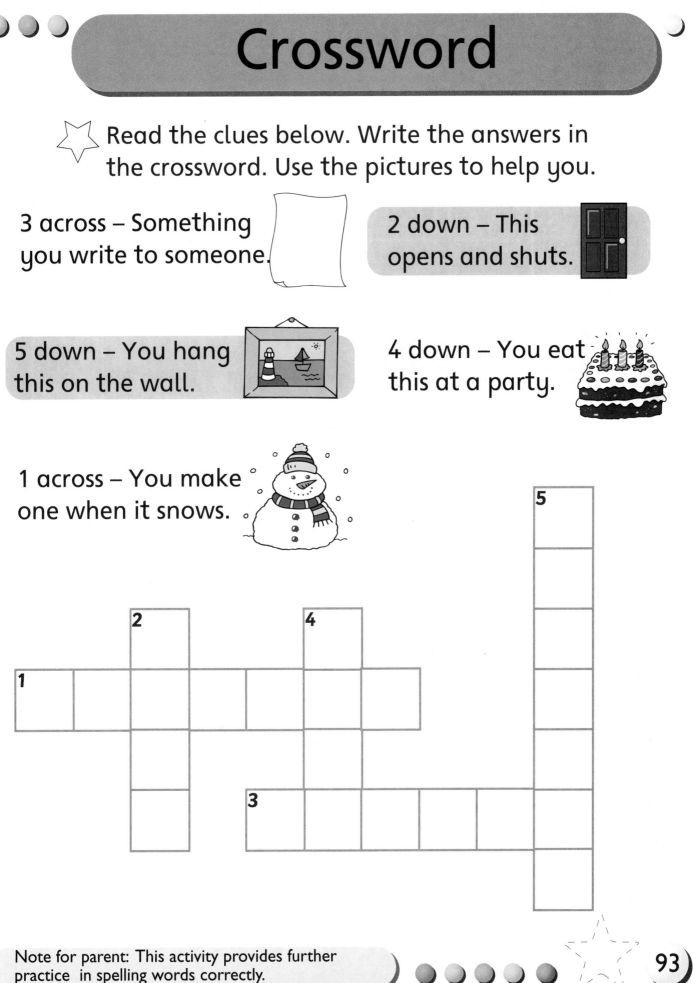

Note for parent: This activity provides further practice in spelling words correctly.

Robots

Read the words. They have the same sound in them, but different spelling patterns. Write each word on the robot with the same spelling pattern. The first one has been done for you.

blow

goal

slow

road

oa

goal

_____

_____

_____

Note for parent: This activity provides practice in understanding that the same middle sounds can be spelled differently.

toad

throw

grow

float

Kites

Read the words. They have the same sound in them, but different spelling patterns. Write each word on the kite with the same spelling pattern.

moon

glue

blue

flew

true

spoon

blew

OO

_____

_____

_____

_____

soon

roof

grew

new

clue

ew

ue

Pizzas

Read the words. They have the same ending sound but they are spelled differently. Write each word on the pizza with the correct spelling. The first one has been done for you.

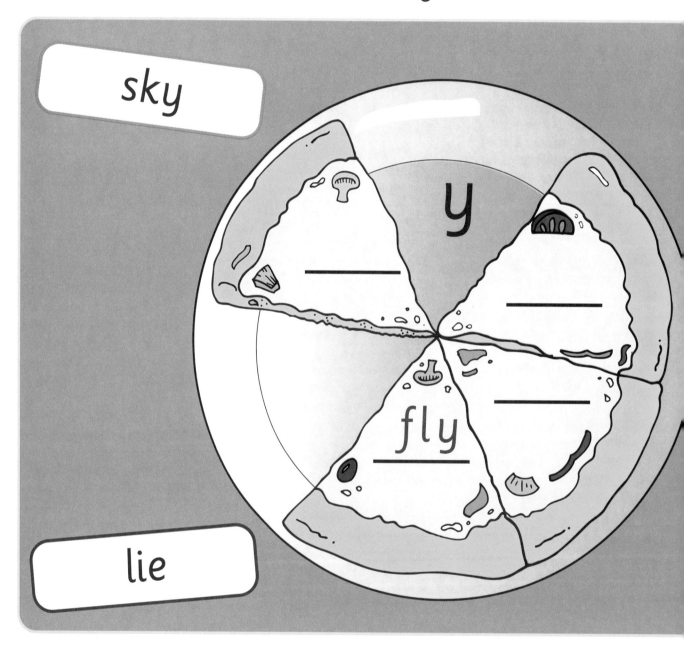

sky

lie

y

fly

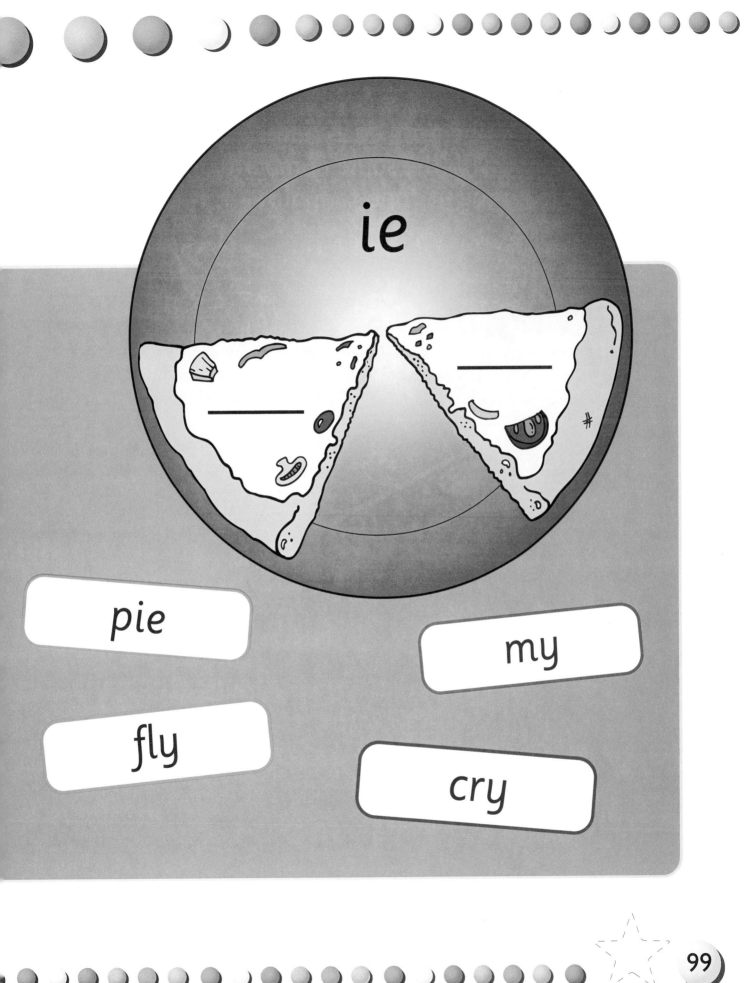

ie

pie

fly

my

cry

Number words

☆ Draw a line from each runner at the top to a runner with the same number word. The first one has been done for you.

two   four   five   one   three

100

Note for parent: This activity provides practice in identifying the spellings of numbers written out as numerals.

6   7   8   9   10

eight   six   ten   seven   nine

Now color the runners on this page.

Doors and keys

☆ Draw lines to join each door to the key with the same number.

11 12 13 14

twelve eleven fourteen fifteen thirteen

⭐ Finish the houses below and color them.

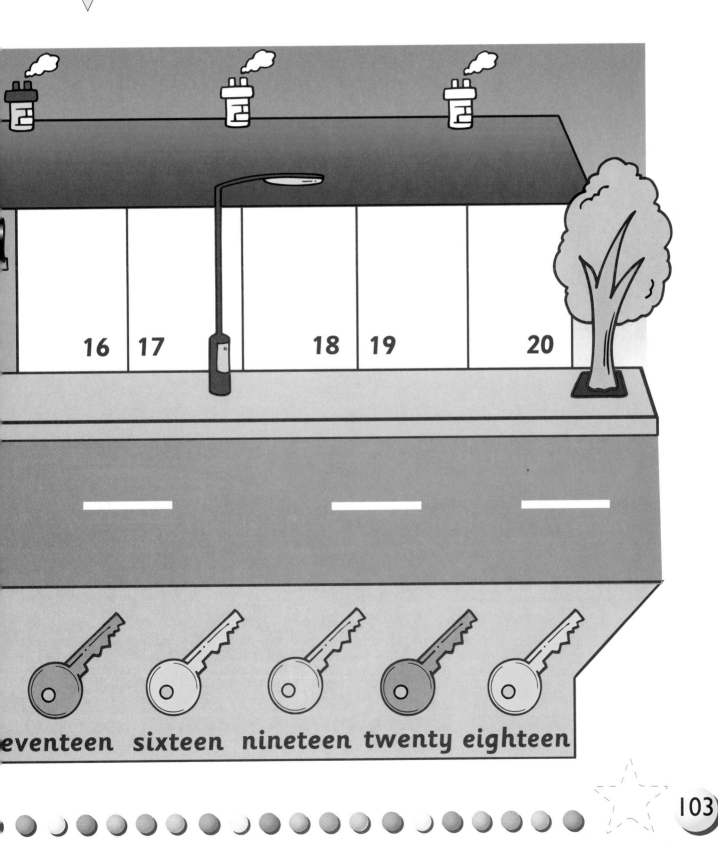

16 17   18 19   20

...eventeen sixteen nineteen twenty eighteen

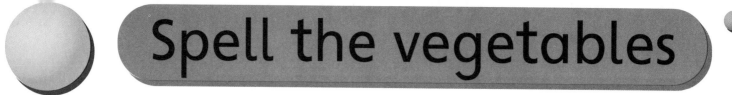

Spell the vegetables

Unscramble the letters to spell the names of the vegetables. Write your answers on the lines.

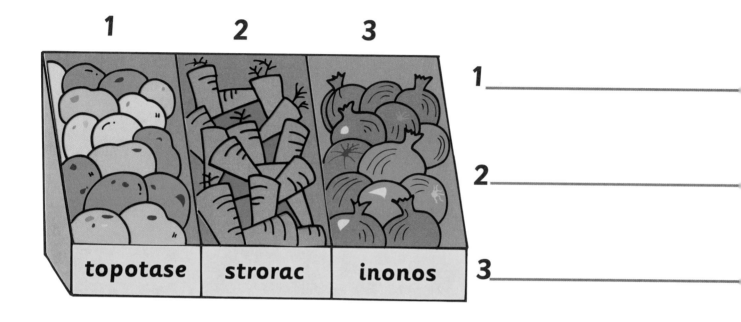

1

2

3

1 topotase

2 strorac

3 inonos

1 _____

2 _____

3 _____

4 _____

5 _____

6 _____

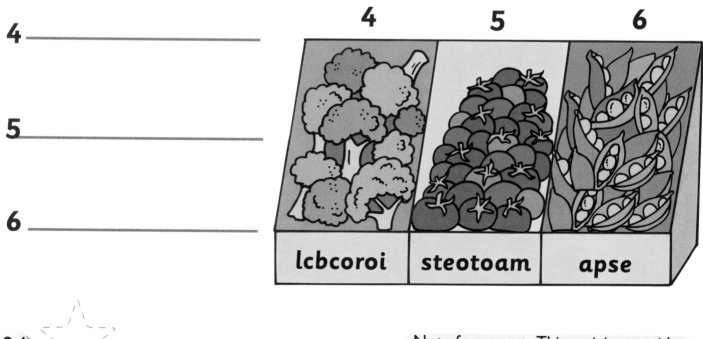

4

5

6

4 lcbcoroi

5 steotoam

6 apse

Note for parent: This activity provides practice in spelling words correctly.

Spell the ingredients

Unscramble the letters to spell the names of the ingredients. Write your answers on the recipe card. Look at the pictures to help you.

ecolcahot

forul

kiml

grsua

ggse

Spell the clothes

⭐ Unscramble the words in the box to find the names of the clothes on the washing line. Write your answers in the spaces.

hrsots sesrd	ajmpaas risht	ejasn cosks

Magic potion

⭐ Unscramble the words in the cauldron to complete the magic potion. Write your answers on the witch's book.

_____ skin

bats' _____

spiders' _____

_____ stools

Name the animals

⭐ Write the names of the animals at the zoo.

seal   monkey
   giraffe
            snake

_____

_____

_____

_____

Note for parent: This activity gives practice in spelling words by labeling objects.

Give each kitten a name. Remember to begin each name with a capital letter. Write the names on the lines in the boxes.

Missing letters

Which letters are missing from each word?
Write them in the spaces.

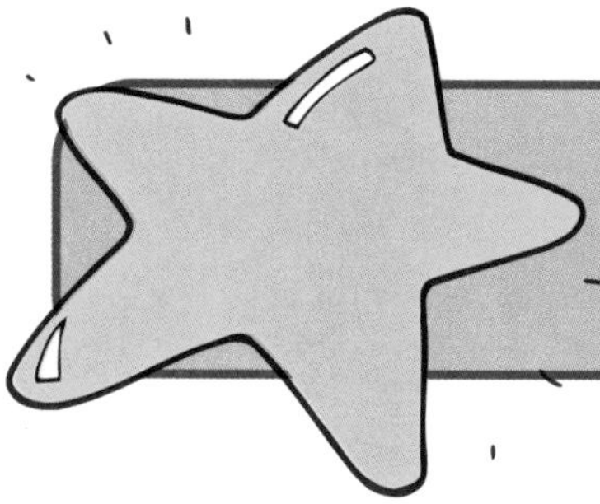

☆ [ ] t [ ] r

m [ ] o [ ]

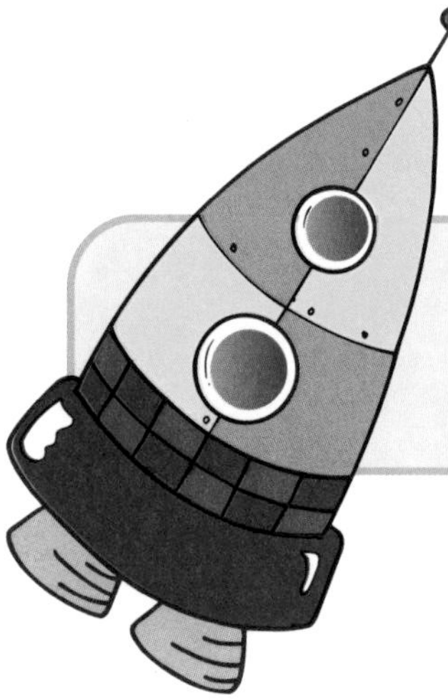

[ ] o c [ ] e t

a [ ] i e [ ]

[ ] l [ ] n [ ] t

Label the car

☆ See if you can label the parts of the car. Write your answers on the lines.

w _____

window   door

wheel   light

l _____

d _____

w _____

☆ Color the picture.

Breakfast time

⭐ Write the names of the objects on the breakfast table.

spoon   juice
toast   cereal

s _____

j _____

t _____

c _____

⭐ What do you like to eat for breakfast?

_____

Label the parts

See if you can label the parts of the head.
Write your answers on the lines.

mouth   eye   nose
hair   ear

h _____

e _____

e _____

n _____

m _____

Read the letters of the alphabet aloud. Write the missing letters in the boxes to complete the alphabet in the sky.

a b c d e f g h i j k l m

Note for parent: This activity gives practice in putting letters into alphabetical order.

o p q r s t u v w x y z

m

y

Join the dots

⭐ Join the dots in order from **a** through **z** to complete the pictures. Then color them.

In the park

⭐ Say each word aloud. Now spell each word aloud.

kite

sky

tree

bench

bird

path

pond

grass

Note for parent: This activity encourages children to develop their memory.

⭐ Cover the facing page. See if you can remember how to spell each object in the picture. Write your answers on the lines.

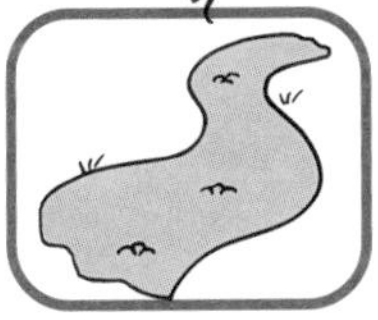

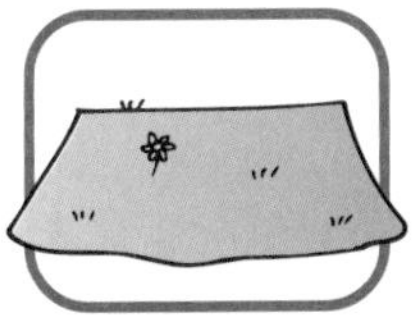

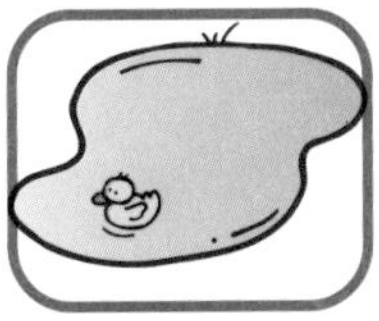

_____

_____

_____

_____

_____

_____

_____

_____

⭐ Now check your answers. Were you right?

At the café

⭐ Say each word aloud. Now spell each word aloud.

pepper

coffee

cake

juice

salt

waiter

chair

table

120

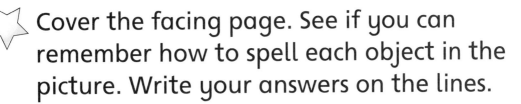

Cover the facing page. See if you can
remember how to spell each object in the
picture. Write your answers on the lines.

_____

_____

_____

_____

_____

_____

_____

_____

Now check your answers. Were you right?

Across and down

Look at each of the pictures. Write the names in the spaces to create a word trail.

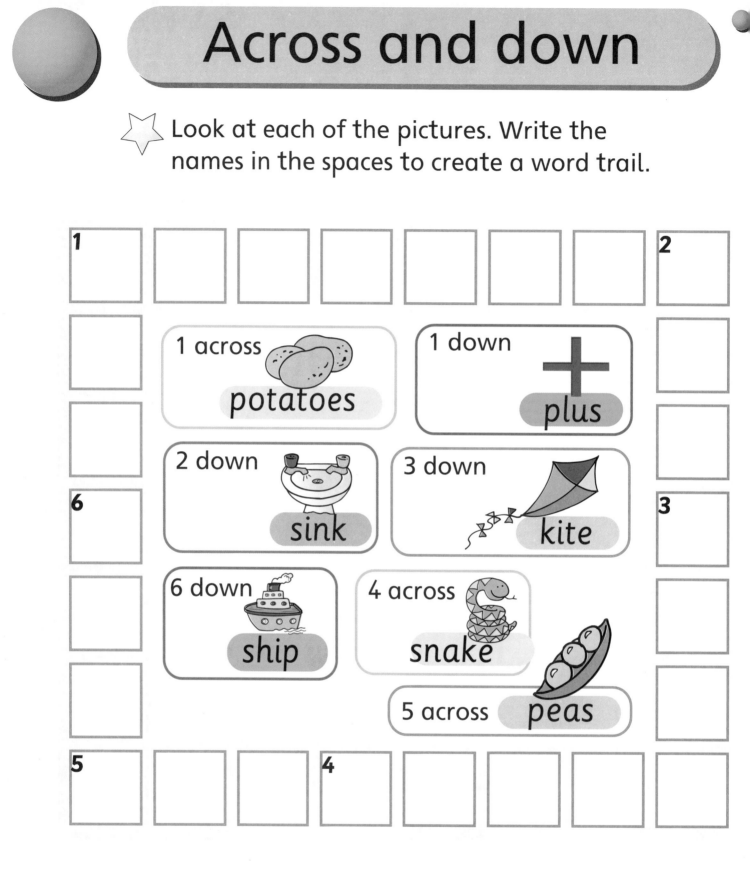

1 across **potatoes**

1 down **plus**

2 down **sink**

3 down **kite**

6 down **ship**

4 across **snake**

5 across **peas**

Note for parent: This activity provides practice in spelling words correctly.

Word puzzle

Read the clues below. Write the words in the crossword. Use the pictures to help you.

1 across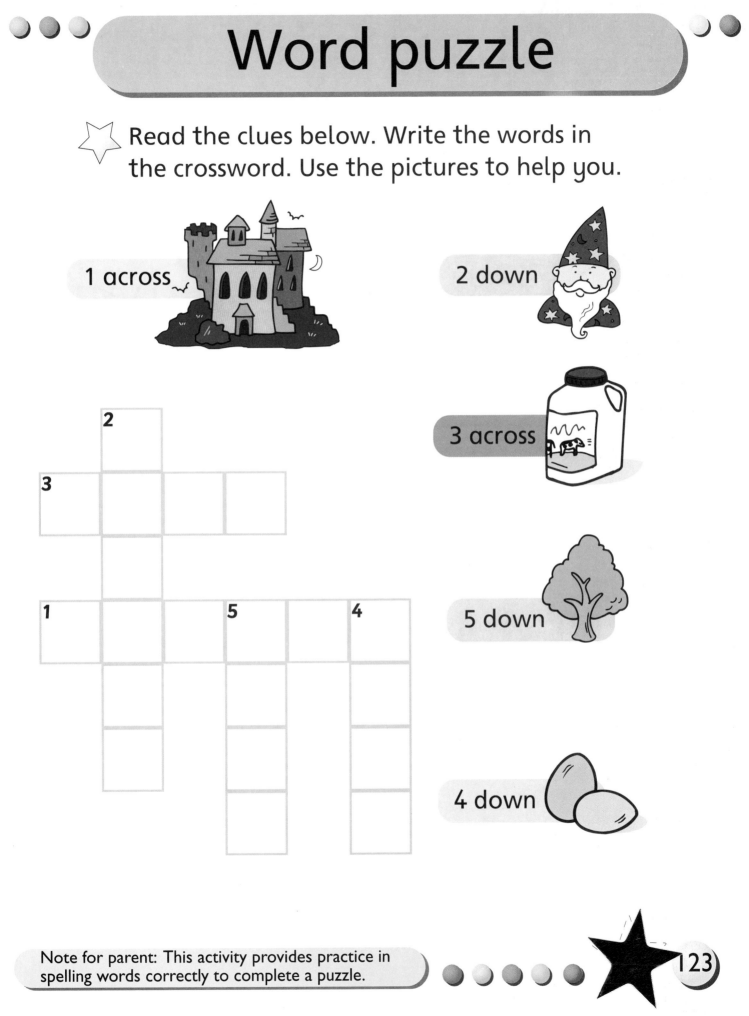

2 down

3 across

5 down

4 down

Note for parent: This activity provides practice in spelling words correctly to complete a puzzle.

123

Correct spellings

★ Look at the pictures and read the words.
Put a ✓next to the correct spelling.

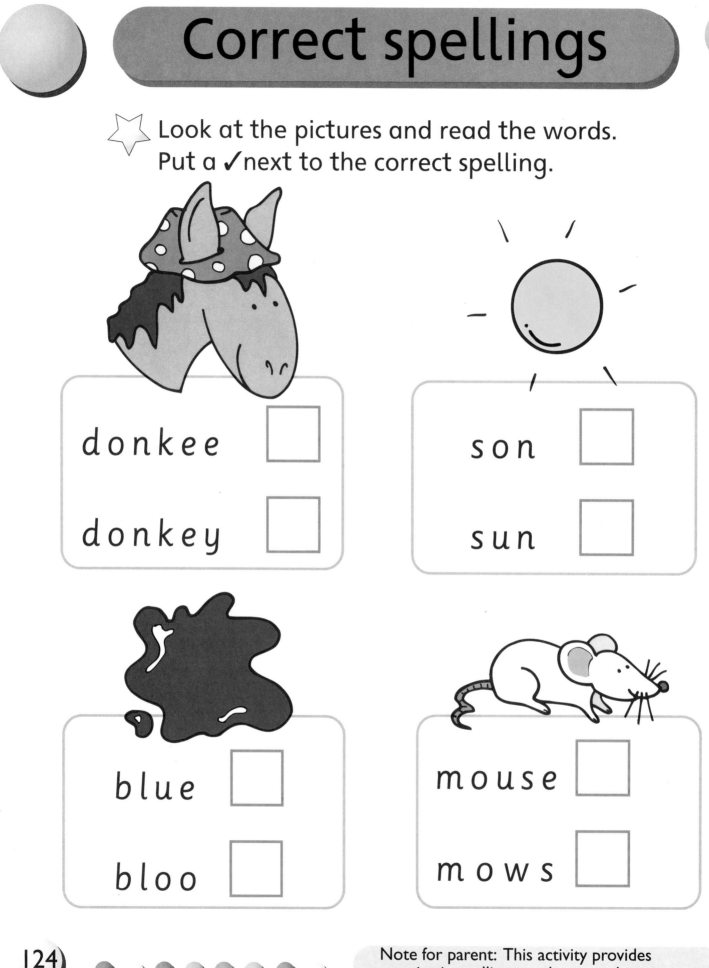

donkee ☐

donkey ☐

son ☐

sun ☐

blue ☐

bloo ☐

mouse ☐

mows ☐

124

Note for parent: This activity provides
practice in spelling words correctly.

shirt ☐

shurt ☐

dear ☐

deer ☐

bear ☐

bare ☐

flower ☐

flour ☐

125

Read each sign on the left. Can you spot the spelling mistakes on each one? Write a new sign with the correct spelling.

wet paind

wet _____

STAP

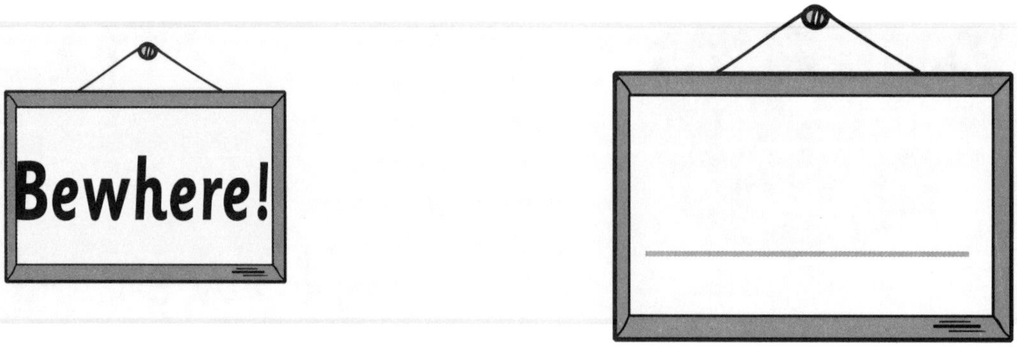

_____

Bewhere!

_____

Toys and Gams

Toys and _____

Road clozed

Road _____

Skool

_____

Ice creem

Ice _____

Peetza

_____

Reading

This section will help with the development and practice of key reading skills. The activities help children to recognize key words by sight and to identify nouns, verbs, and adjectives. They also encourage skills such as observation and storytelling.

In the toystore

Look carefully at the picture of the toystore.
Can you spot the things in the list below?
Circle each one you find.

1 Two things that begin with the letter **r** .

2 Two things that begin with the letter **t.**

3 Two things that begin with the letter **d.**

4 Two things that do not belong in the toystore.

Choose the word

Choose the correct word in the middle of each sentence. Draw a ring around it.

1 Butterflies **have** / **eat** two wings.

2 The children **swim** / **play** in the park.

3 The cat **barks** / **meows** at the dog.

4 Dad **washes** / **paints** the car.

5 The mailman **rings** / **bites** the doorbell.

6 I have **books** / **cereal** for breakfast.

7 The mouse **eats** / **is** the cheese.

8 There are **stars** / **cars** in the sky.

9 Penguins **swim** / **run** in the water.

10 The train is **going** / **hopping** to town.

11 I wear **slippers** / **mittens** on my feet.

Nouns

Words that name people, animals, things, and places are called nouns. Write these nouns in the correct list.

girl   cat   doctor

mug   rabbit   t-shirt

people

_____

_____

things

_____

_____

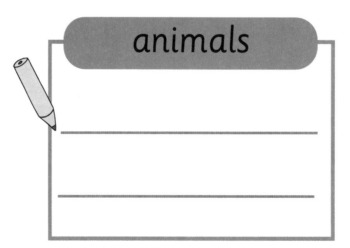

animals

_____

_____

Write the names of towns or countries you have visited. Remember to start each name with a capital letter.
We have done an example for you.

<u>Scotland</u>

_____

_____

Write a list of people you know. Remember to start each name with a capital letter. We have done an example for you.

<u>Mr Jones</u>

_____

_____

_____

What I do

Fill in the missing words to say what each person does. Use the words in the box to help you. Read the completed sentences.

cook   drive

bake   build   grow

teach   check

I _____ food.

I _____ houses.

I _____ the bus.

I _____ bread.

I _____ children.

I _____ teeth.

I _____ vegetables.

A verb tells us what someone or something is doing. Read each sentence. Circle the verb in each sentence. The first one has been done for you.

The monkey (climbs) up the tree.

The kangaroo jumps along.

The frog hops out of the pond.

The duck paddles in in the pond.

The dog wags his tail.

Playing

Look at the pictures. Put a ✓ next to the verb that describes what each child is doing. The first one has been done for you.

sliding ☐
kicking ✓

digging ☐
sliding ☐

swinging ☐
flying ☐

swinging ☐
digging ☐

kicking ☐
digging ☐

Verbs in a day

⭐ Read the sentences below. Circle the verb in each sentence. The first one has been done for you.

Becky (eats) cereal and toast for breakfast.

She rides her bike to the park.

Becky plays on the swings in the park.

She makes a cheese sandwich for lunch.

Becky watches TV in the afternoon.

She puts her toys away in her bedroom.

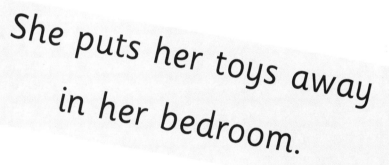

Becky reads her book in bed.

Which word?

Read what the children are saying.
Write the correct word in each space to
complete the sentences.

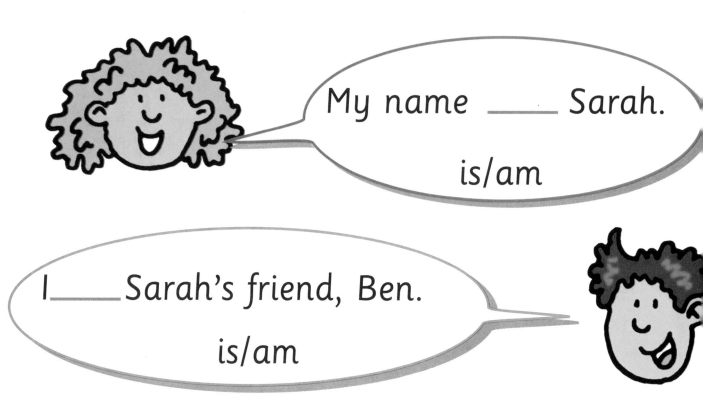

My name ____ Sarah.

is/am

I____ Sarah's friend, Ben.

is/am

Sarah and Ben

____ going to the

library.

is/are

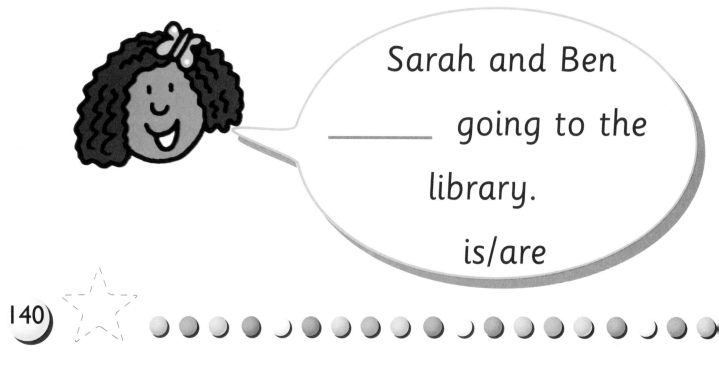

At the pool

Look at the picture. Read the sentences.
Circle the correct verb in each sentence.

1 The children **is** / **are** at the swimming pool.

2 The girl **is** / **are** standing by the pool.

3 The boys **is** / **are** swimming.

4 The instructor **is** / **are** blowing a whistle.

Describing

Look at each of the pictures. Draw a line from each picture to the correct word that describes it.

happy

sad

clever

helpful

sleepy

Look at the picture. Read the questions. Put a ✓ next to the correct answer.

		yes	no
1	Is the girl's hair curly?	☐	☐
2	Is the kite red?	☐	☐
3	Is it sunny?	☐	☐
4	Is the girl sad?	☐	☐

Describe the objects

Which word describes each object? Circle the correct word.

happy   /   shiny

fluffy   /   hard

comfortable   /sad

hot   /   cold

old   /   cute

Note for parent: This activity provides practice in identifying and writing adjectives.

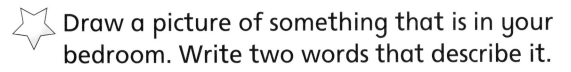 Draw a picture of something that is in your bedroom. Write two words that describe it.

Describe the animals

Look at each animal. Choose the word that describes it. Circle the correct word.

green   big

fluffy   smooth

furry   slow

cold   little

stripy   spotty

Draw a picture of your favorite animal. Put a ✓ next to the words that describe it. You can tick more than one box.

big ☐   thin ☐   hairy ☐

small ☐   gentle ☐   slippery ☐

fat ☐   smooth ☐   long ☐

Spot the difference

⭐ Look carefully at the two pictures. How many differences can you spot in the bottom picture? Circle each one you find.

⭐ Read and complete this sentence:

I found _____ differences.

Note for parent: This activity encourages observation.

Read and draw

Draw a ladybug next to each flower.

Draw 4 leaves on the pink flower.

Color the caterpillar.

Draw 2 petals on the red flower.

⭐ Look at each picture. Read the sentences carefully. Circle the correct sentence that describes the picture.

a The clown is making the children sad.

b The clown is making the children happy.

c The clown is making the children sleepy.

a The little boy is holding a balloon.

b The little girl is eating ice cream.

c The little boy is eating ice cream.

a The cat is watching two fish.

b The dog is watching two fish.

c The cat is watching three fish.

In the jungle

Look at the picture. Write a sentence saying what each animal is doing. Read your sentences aloud.

_____

_____

_____

_____

_____

_____

_____

_____

Penguin pictures

⭐ Look at the pictures. Write a sentence about each picture. Read your sentences aloud to an adult.

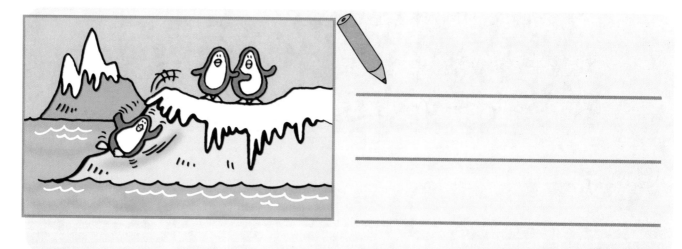

 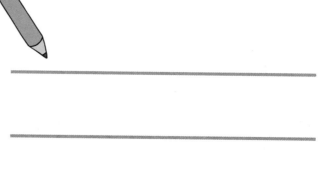

What do you think happens next? Write your ideas on the lines. Read your sentences aloud. Then draw a picture in the box.

Reading aloud

⭐ Look at the picture. What do you think happens next? Write your answers on the lines. Then read your answers aloud to an adult.

Look at the picture. What do you think happens next? Write your answers on the lines. Then read your answers aloud to an adult.

Magazine covers

⭐ Look at the magazine cover. Which story is about keeping fit? Draw a ring around it.
Which story is about pop stars? Put a tick next to it.

⭐ What do you think the other stories are about?

_____

_____

Note for parent: This activity looks at different kinds of reading material.

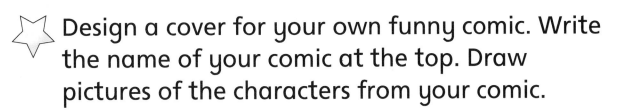

Design a cover for your own funny comic. Write the name of your comic at the top. Draw pictures of the characters from your comic.

Book fun

Look at the picture on each book. Write a title that describes what each book is about.

This book is called

_____

_____

This book is called

_____

_____

Note for parent: This activity encourages children to think about covers and the content of books.

⭐ What is the name of your favorite book?

✏️ _____

My favorite book is about _____

_____

I like it because_____

⭐ Draw a
picture of
its cover.

Which shelf?

 Look at the three shelves below. On which shelf do the newspaper, the magazine, and the comic belong? Write your answers in the boxes.

newspaper   magazine   comic

☐   ☐   ☐

a

b

c

Note for parent: This activity looks at different kinds of reading material.

Look at the three shelves of books. Where do the books below belong? Write the shelf numbers in the boxes.

animals
☐

science
☐

mystery
☐

shelf 1

shelf 2

shelf 3

Look and find

Look carefully at the two pictures. Can you find 7 differences in the bottom one? Circle each one you find

Note for parent: This activity encourages observation.

Color word search

Can you find these colors in the word search? The words read across, down, diagonally, and up.

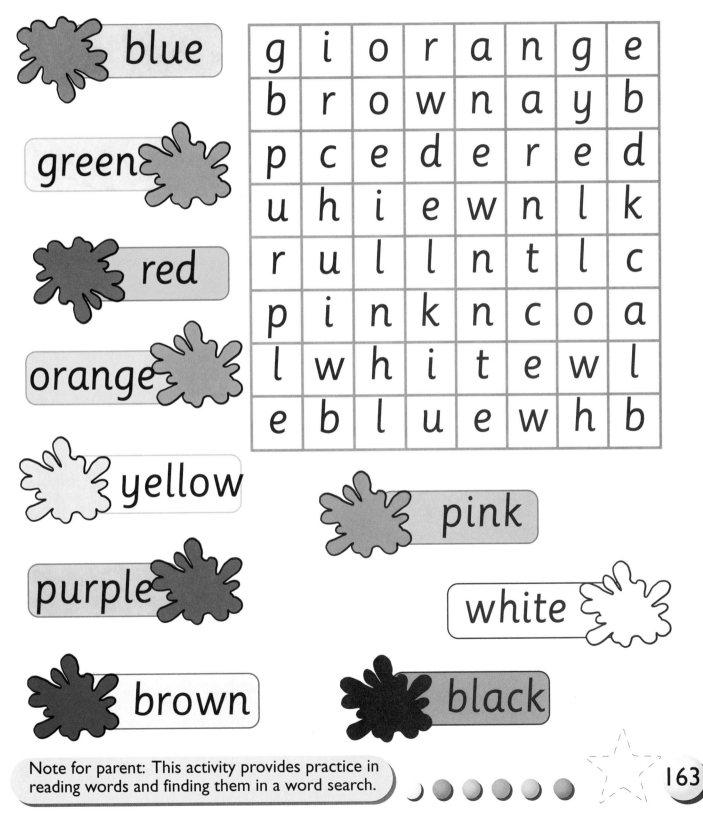

blue

green

red

orange

yellow

pink

purple

white

brown

black

g	i	o	r	a	n	g	e
b	r	o	w	n	a	y	b
p	c	e	d	e	r	e	d
u	h	i	e	w	n	l	k
r	u	l	l	n	t	l	c
p	i	n	k	n	c	o	a
l	w	h	i	t	e	w	l
e	b	l	u	e	w	h	b

What is in the bag?

⭐ Read the list of what is in each school bag.

Bag 1

1 book
2 pens
paper
1 workbook

Bag 2

1 pencil case
lunch
2 books
stickers

Bag 3

3 pens
2 books
paper
lunch
keys

⭐ Read and answer these questions.
Write the correct bag number in each box.

1 Which bag has keys?

2 Which bags have 2 books?

3 Which bag has a workbook?

4 Which bags have pens?

5 Which bag has a pencil case?

What do you have in your school bag? Write a list. Remember when you write a list to put the items one under another.

Now read your list aloud.

Going on vacation

Sam and Mary are going on vacation.
Read what they have in their suitcases.

Sam

4 t-shirts
2 sweaters
2 pairs of jeans
3 shorts
swimming trunks
shoes
jacket
socks
underwear
blue sunglasses

Mary

2 shirts
3 t-shirts
1 dress
underwear
1 pair of jeans
2 shorts
swimsuit
jacket
shoes
socks
yellow sunglasses

Answer the questions below.
Put a ✓ under the correct suitcase.

Sam   Mary

1 Who packed 1 pair of jeans?

2 Who packed blue sunglasses?

3 Who packed 4 t-shirts?

4 Who packed 2 shirts?

⭐ Read Sam and Mary's plans for their first day.

08:00	**Have breakfast**
09:00	**Go to the museum**
11:00	**Take a walk along the river**
12:30	**Have lunch**
02:15	**Go for a swim at the pool**
03:30	**Play games**
05:00	**Get dressed for dinner**

⭐ Read the questions. Write your answers on the lines.

1 What time are they going for a swim?

_____

2 What are they doing at 09:00?

_____

3 What are they doing just before lunch?

_____

Read the labels on the pet foods. Draw a line to join each food to the correct animal.

Note for parent: This activity provides practice in reading signs.

Read the poster

Look at the poster. Read the questions.
Write your answers on the lines.

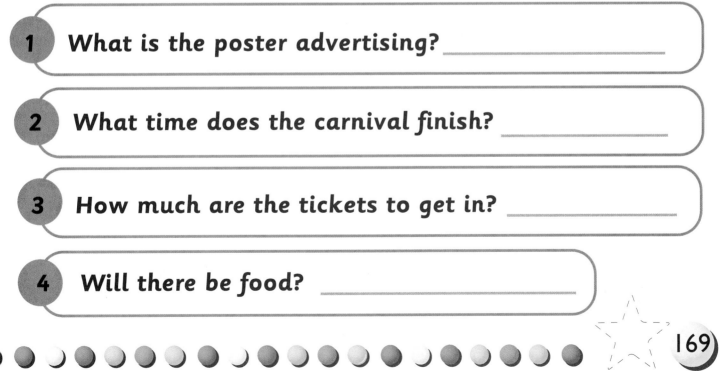

1 **What is the poster advertising?** _____

2 **What time does the carnival finish?** _____

3 **How much are the tickets to get in?** _____

4 **Will there be food?** _____

In my bedroom

Read the sentences and finish the picture.

1 Draw a pillow on the bed.
2 Draw 2 toys in the toy box.
3 Color the rug on the floor.
4 Color the lamp on the desk.
5 Draw a book on the desk.

Silly supermarket

There are some silly things happening in the supermarket. Read the sentences. Put a ✓ to say if they are true or false.

		true	false
1	The clown is juggling fruit.	☐	☐
2	There are 2 giraffes in the supermarket.	☐	☐
3	A king is pushing a shopping cart.	☐	☐
4	A man is lying on a skateboard.	☐	☐
5	The deep-sea diver is holding 3 fish.	☐	☐

Cat and mouse

The mouse eats the cheese

The mouse sees a piece of cheese.

The cat chases the mouse.

The dog chases the cat.

Note for parent: This activity encourages children to observe and to put pictures in the right order to tell a story.

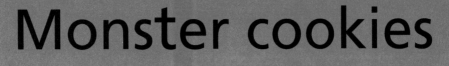

Put the pictures in order from 1 through 4 to tell the story. Write the numbers in the boxes.

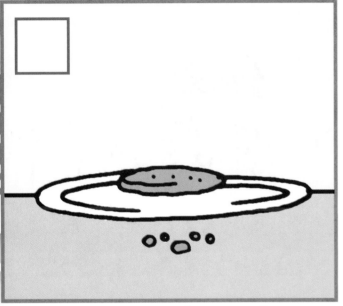

Who is eating the cookies?

Now there are only three.

A monster has eaten all the cookies!

There is a full plate of cookies.

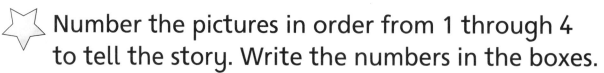

Number the pictures in order from 1 through 4 to tell the story. Write the numbers in the boxes.

The wizard looks in his book for a special brew.

"Perfect brew," he says

Then he casts the spell.

He mixes the ingredients.

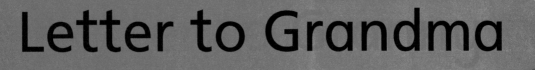

Letter to Grandma

Number the pictures in order from 1 through 6 to tell the story. Write the numbers in the boxes.

Grandma loves her drawing!

Then he mails it.

A little boy draws a picture for his Grandma.

The mailman collects it from the mail box.

He puts the picture in an envelope.

Another mailman delivers it.

Six differences

Look carefully at the two pictures. Can you spot the 6 differences in the bottom picture? Circle each one you find.

Note for parent: This activity encourages observation.

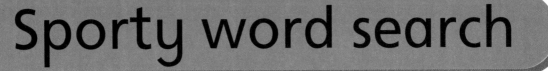

Sporty word search

⭐ Can you find these sports in the word search? The words read across and down.

tennis   football
basketball   soccer   softball
running   baseball

b	a	s	k	e	t	b	a	l	l
a	f	o	e	t	r	u	g	d	y
s	o	f	s	r	u	g	b	a	l
e	o	t	t	e	n	n	i	s	k
b	t	b	t	e	n	n	s	o	e
a	b	a	c	d	i	c	k	c	t
l	a	l	m	i	n	t	o	c	b
l	l	l	i	n	g	b	y	e	a
g	l	i	b	a	l	l	f	r	l

Note for parent: This activity gives practice in reading words and finding them in a word search.

177

⭐ Look carefully at the picture below.
Read the signs in the park.

Note for parent: This activity encourages children to read instructions carefully.

Answer the questions below. Put a ✔ in the correct box to show if you can do these things in the park.

Can you feed the ducks?

yes   no

Can you ride a bicycle?

yes   no

Can you swim in the pond?

yes   no

Can you put garbage in the trash can?

yes   no

Words and pictures

Read the sentences below. Draw a line to join each picture with the correct group of sentences.

1 A girl has a yellow balloon. One boy has a red balloon. The other boy has a blue balloon.

2 A boy has a blue balloon One girl has a yellow balloon. The other girl has a red balloon.

3 A boy has a red balloon. One girl has a blue balloon. Another girl has a yellow balloon.

4 A boy has a yellow balloon. Another boy has a red balloon. A girl has a blue balloon.

Note for parent: This activity encourages children to read carefully and to follow instructions.

Fill in the calendar

Read the sentences below and draw the correct pictures on the calendar.

Calendar

Monday	Tuesday	Wednesday
Thursday	**Friday**	**Saturday**
		Sunday

1. Dad is going fishing on Tuesday. Draw a fish on the calendar.
2. It's your sister's birthday on Friday. Draw a gift on the calendar.
3. Your friend is coming over to play on Monday. Draw a picture of your friend on the calendar.
4. The circus is coming on Sunday. Draw a funny clown on the calendar.

When Molly goes home from school, she passes 5 houses, a park, and 3 stores. Which way does Molly go home? Circle the correct letter.

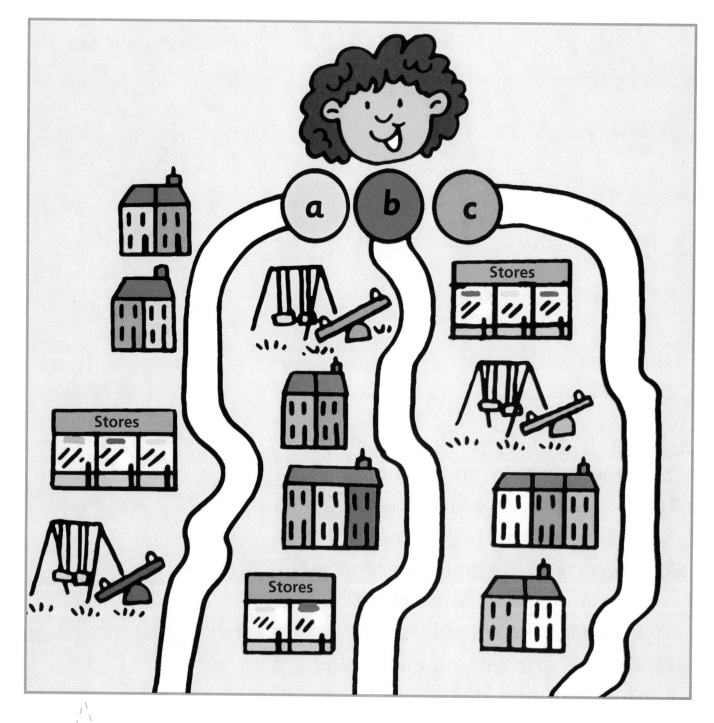

Wizard magic

The wizard needs your help with a magic potion.
Put a ✔ next to the ingredients he already has.
Put a ✘ next to the ones where something is missing.

eyes of frogs

bats' wings

swamp gas

false teeth

green slime

frogs' legs

7 eyes of frog	
6 bats' wings	
swamp gas	
4 false teeth	
green slime	

It's party time!

⭐ Read the sentences and then finish the picture.

1. Draw a plate to the left of each napkin.

2. Draw a pizza in the middle of the table.

3. Draw a dog to the left of the empty chair.

4. Draw a person in the empty chair.

Find the fruits

Can you find all the fruit words in the word search? Circle each one you find. The words read across, down, up diagonally, and backward.

grapefruit   pineapple   melon

strawberry   blueberry   raspberry

g	p	i	n	e	a	p	p	l	e
s	r	r	f	b	c	a	b	m	t
t	i	a	o	l	a	v	l	e	l
r	c	e	p	u	o	n	k	l	e
a	p	p	l	e	b	s	a	o	g
w	e	t	w	b	f	c	w	n	n
b	a	r	y	e	t	r	c	e	a
e	c	h	e	r	r	y	u	m	r
r	h	l	f	r	h	m	b	i	o
r	a	g	g	y	b	p	e	d	t
y	r	r	e	b	p	s	a	r	x

banana

apple

cherry

peach

pear

orange

185

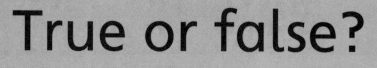

True or false?

Look at the picture. Read the sentences. Put a ✓ in the boxes to say whether the sentences are true or false.

	true	false
1 The girl is 5 today.	☐	☐
2 There are 3 boys at the party.	☐	☐
3 There are 7 presents on the floor.	☐	☐
4 There is a pizza on the table.	☐	☐

☆ Write about your last birthday. Did you have a party? What presents did you get?

_____

_____

_____

_____

☆ Now read aloud what you have written.

Fun at the fair

⭐ Look carefully at the picture. Then answer the questions.

1 Is the roller-coaster going up or down?

_____

2 Where is the girl's ice cream?

_____

3 Who wants to eat the girl's ice cream?

_____

4 How many people are on the
   roller-coaster?

_____

5 What is the prize for the ball game?

_____

6 How many balls is the juggler juggling?

_____

Days of the week

Read the sentences below. Can you work out the correct days? Write your answers on the lines.

WEEKDAYS

Monday

Tuesday

Wednesday

Thursday

Friday

WEEKEND

Saturday

Sunday

1. Lisa went shopping the day after Monday. On which day did she go shopping?

_____

2. Peter played football the day before Sunday. On which day did he play football?

_____

3. Bill starts school on the first day after the weeke On which day does he start school?

_____

4. Maria is going to visit her grandma this weekend On which days will she visit her?

_____

5. Today is Tuesday. Nick is going to the movies the day after tomorrow. On which day is he going to the movies?

_____

Jokes

Read each of the jokes. Draw a line to join each question to its punchline.

1 How do you start a teddy bear race?

a Palm trees.

2 What trees do fingers and thumbs grow on?

b Ice-cream man.

3 What kind of person has a very loud voice?

c A bulldozer.

d Ready, teddy, go.

4 What do you call a sleeping cow?

Math

The activities in this section will help children to develop and practice key math skills. The activities include simple measuring, shape recognition, and telling the time. They also provide practice in tables and addition, subtraction, and multiplication.

Tape measure

Use the tape measure to help you work out the measurements. Write your answers in the boxes. The first one has been done for you.

1 2 3 4 5 6 7 8 9 10 11 12 13 14 15 16 17 18 19 20

Start at 3. Count forward 4. **7**

Start at 9. Count forward 6.

Start at 11. Count forward 4.

Start at 12. Count forward 8.

Start at 20. Count back 4.

Start at 19. Count back 10.

Start at 10. Count back 7.

Start at 12. Count back 3. Count forward 5.

Start at 15. Count forward 5. Count back 10.

Note for parent: This activity introduces children to measuring.

Using a ruler

Use this inch (in) ruler to help you measure the lines. Put your finger at the end of each line. Then follow it up to the ruler.
Write the numbers in the boxes. The first one has been done for you.

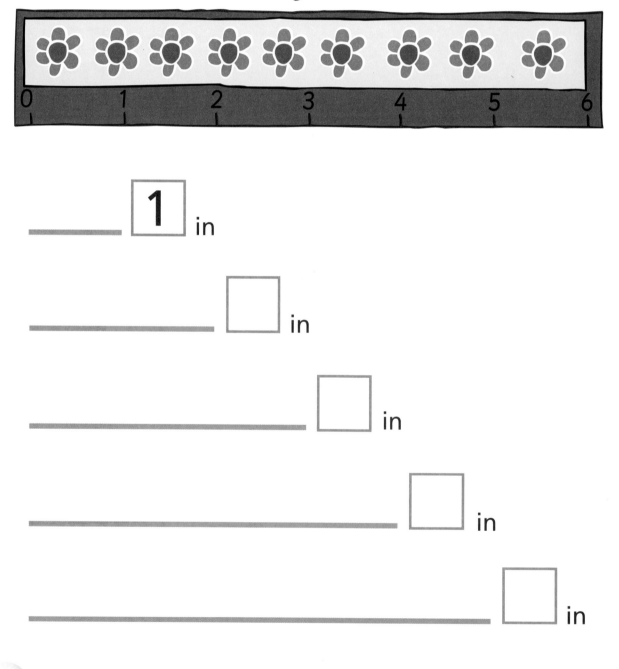

1	in
	in
	in
	in
	in

Note for parent: This activity provides further practice with measuring.

Find a ruler and measure these objects. Write the answers in the boxes.

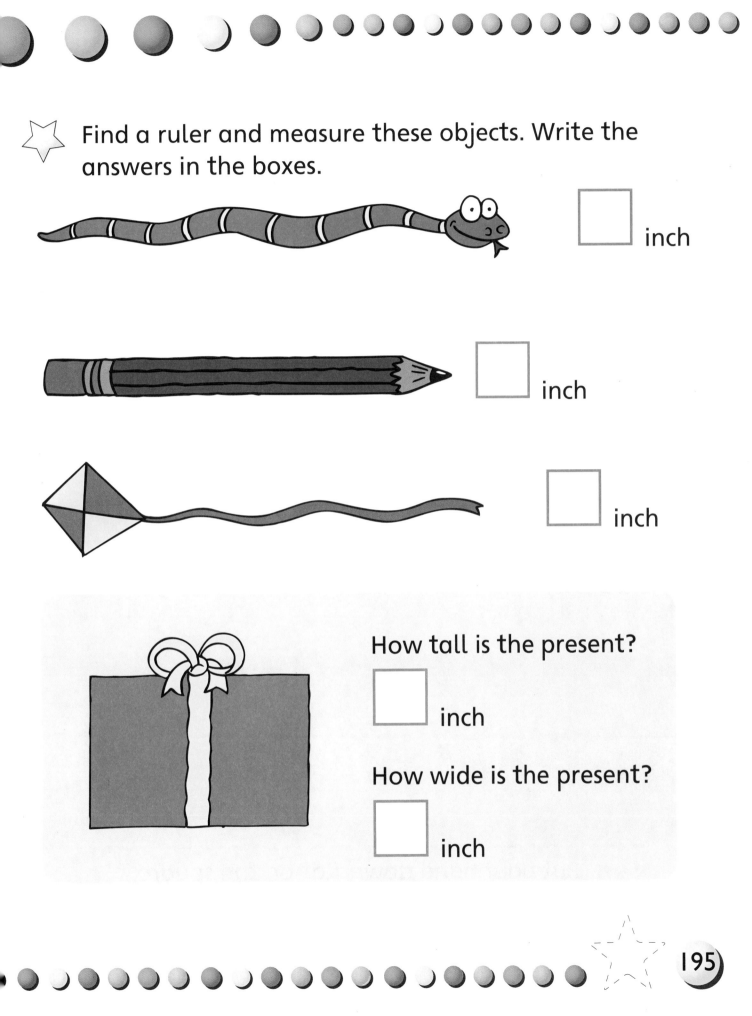

☐ inch

☐ inch

☐ inch

How tall is the present?

☐ inch

How wide is the present?

☐ inch

Hand spans

Your hand span is the distance from your pinkie to your thumb.

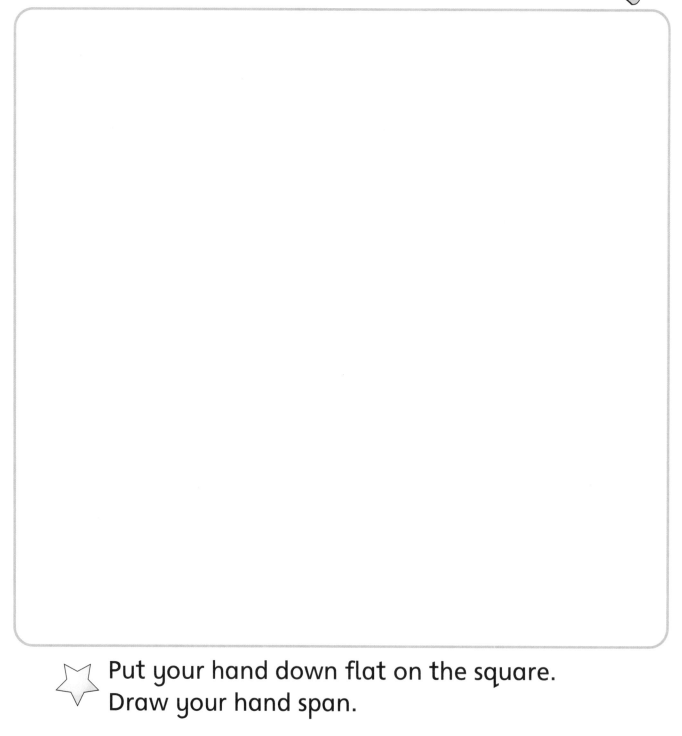

Put your hand down flat on the square. Draw your hand span.

⭐ Now measure objects in your home using your hand span. Write your answers in the boxes.

a pillow

a table

a window

spans

spans

spans

a television

a door

spans

spans

2-D shapes

Flat shapes are called two-dimensional shapes, or 2-D shapes for short. Say the names of these 2-D shapes aloud.

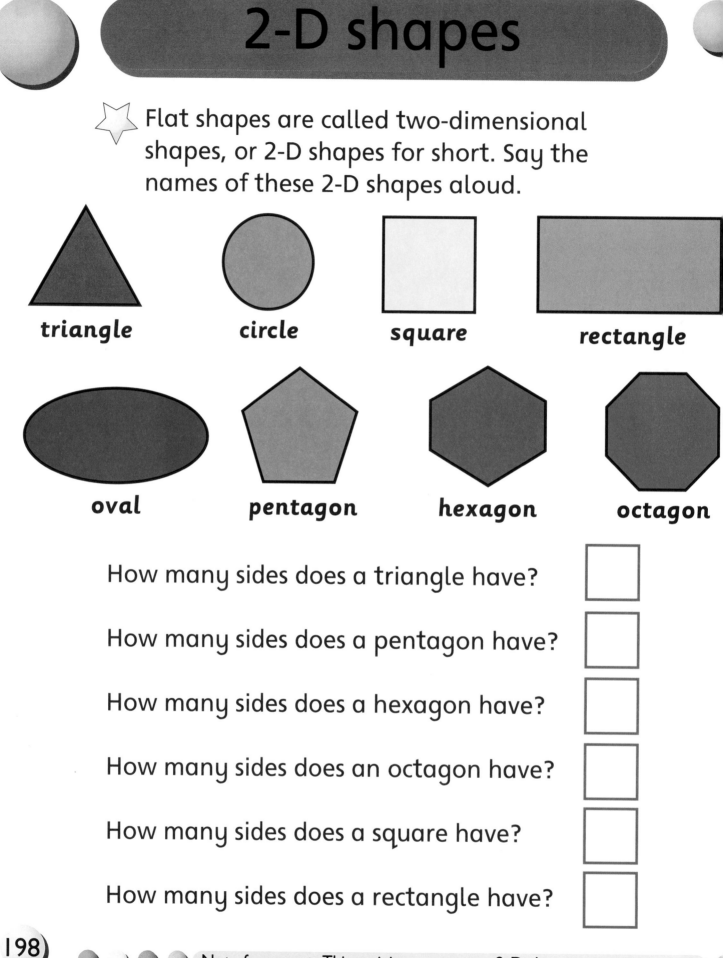

triangle **circle** **square** **rectangle**

oval **pentagon** **hexagon** **octagon**

How many sides does a triangle have? ☐

How many sides does a pentagon have? ☐

How many sides does a hexagon have? ☐

How many sides does an octagon have? ☐

How many sides does a square have? ☐

How many sides does a rectangle have? ☐

⭐ Can you answer these questions about 2-D shapes? Write your answers on the lines.

A square and a rectangle both have 4 sides. How are they different?

_____

How is an oval different from a circle?

_____

⭐ Can you spot all the 2-D shapes in this picture? Color each one you find.

Making objects

 Draw petals around
the circle to make
a flower.

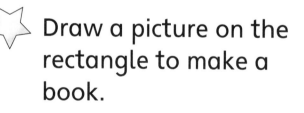 Draw some curtains in the
square to make a window.

Draw a picture on the
rectangle to make a
book.

 200

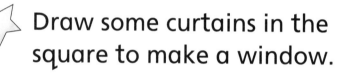

Note for parent: This activity encourages 2-D shape recognition.

⭐ Draw holes in the triangle to make a piece of cheese.

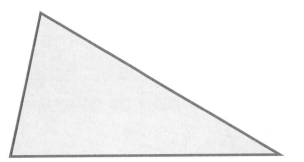

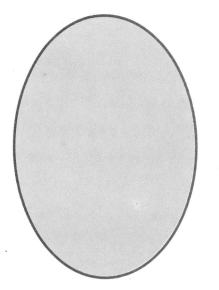

⭐ Draw 2 eyes, a mouth and a nose in the oval to make a face. Draw on some hair.

⭐ What can you draw on this pentagon? What object does it turn into? Write your answer on the line.

_____

3-D shapes

⭐ All these shapes are three-dimensional shapes, or 3-D shapes for short. Say the names of each shape aloud.

sphere

prism

cube

cone

cylinder

⭐ Which 2-D shapes can you see in the 3-D shapes? Draw the 2-D shapes below each 3-D shape.

Note for parent: This activity encourages 3-D shape recognition.

Look at the objects below. Which 3-D shapes are they?

Put a ✔ in the correct boxes.

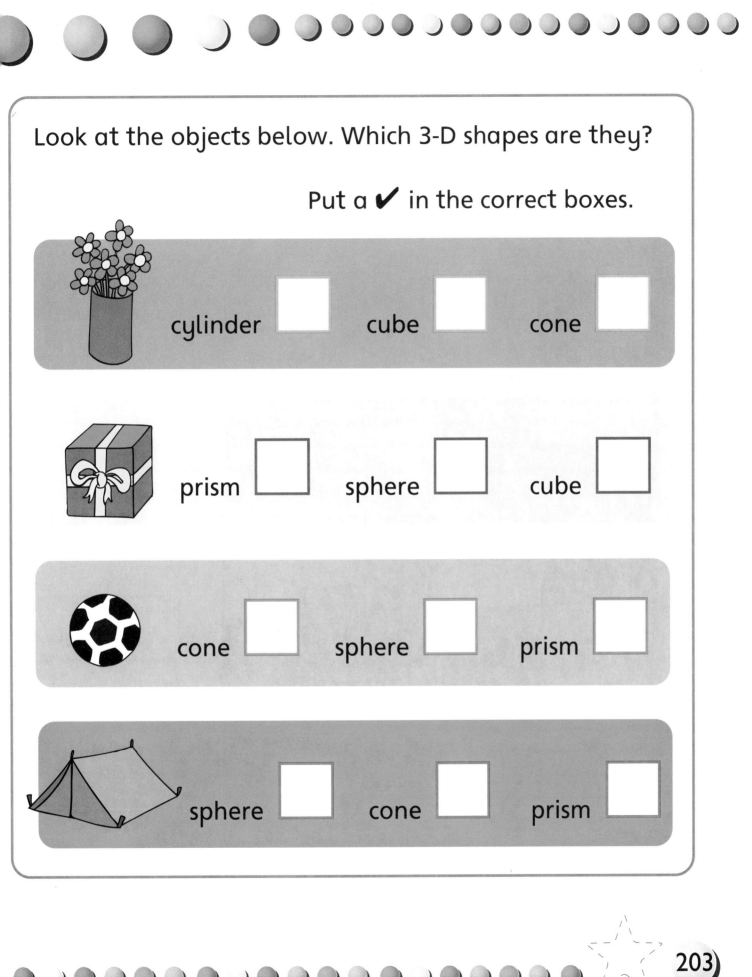

cylinder ☐   cube ☐   cone ☐

prism ☐   sphere ☐   cube ☐

cone ☐   sphere ☐   prism ☐

sphere ☐   cone ☐   prism ☐

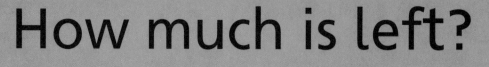

☆ Look at the foods on the picnic blanket. How much of each food is left? Draw a line from each one to the word that describes how much is left.

half

whole

half-full

empty

full

Note for parent: This activity introduces words used to describe measurements.

Sizes

☆ Color the tallest house red. Color the smallest house green.

☆ Color the shortest sock blue.

☆ Put the worms in order, from shortest through longest. Number them from 1 through 3.

☆ Put the animals in order, from lightest through heaviest. Number them from 1 through 3.

More on sizes

⭐ Look at the objects in each row. Draw a ring around the smallest one.

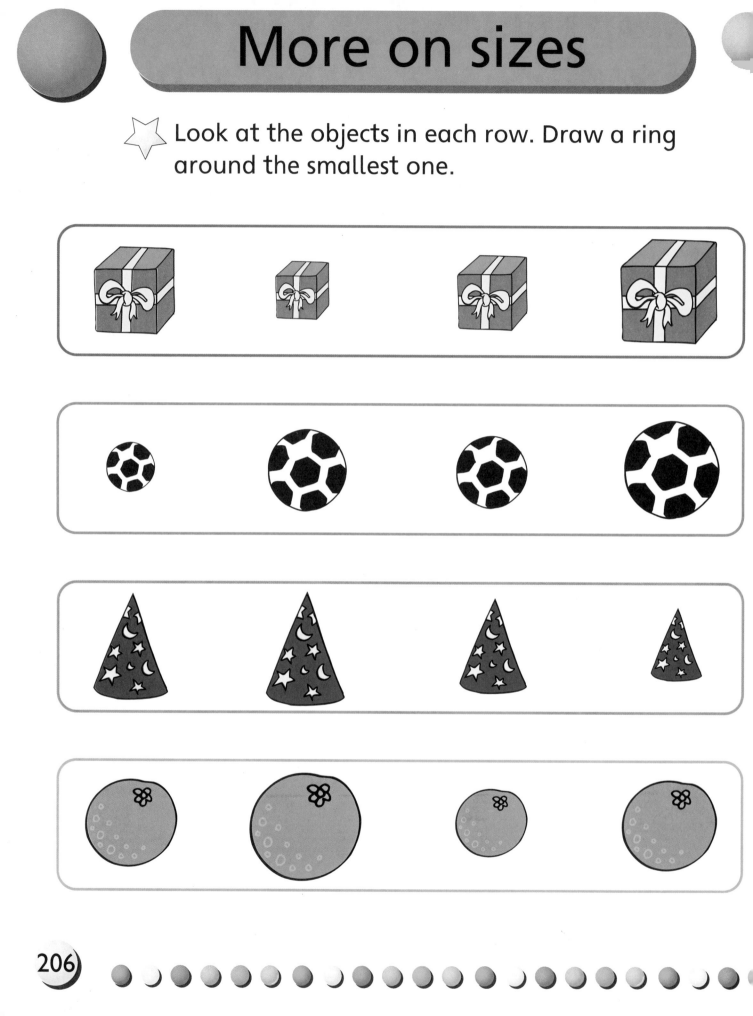

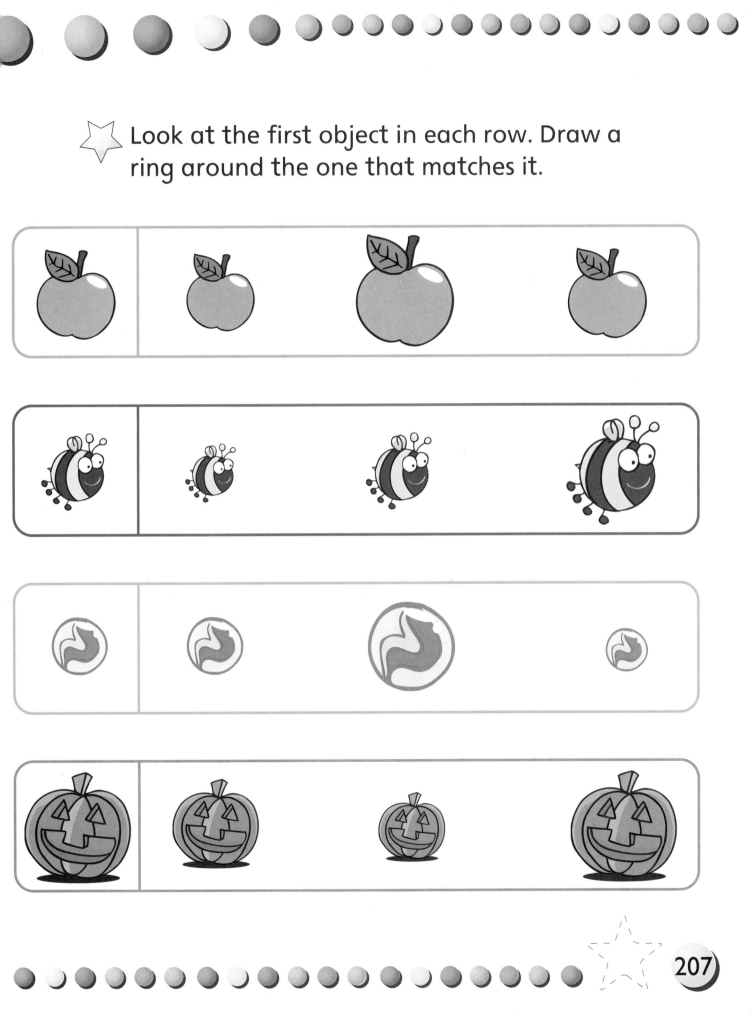

Look at the first object in each row. Draw a
ring around the one that matches it.

Shape patterns

Look at the patterns of 2-D shapes below. Trace over the dotted lines of the correct shape that comes next in each row.

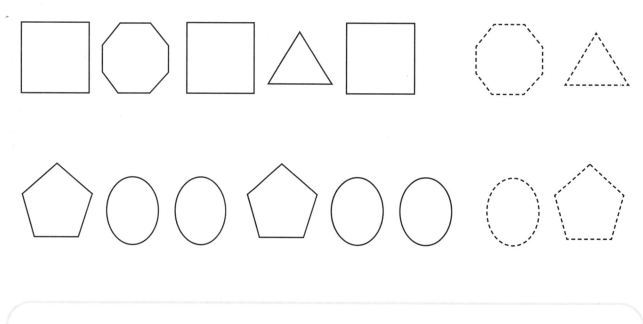

Look at the 3-D objects below. Draw a line to join each shape to its correct name.

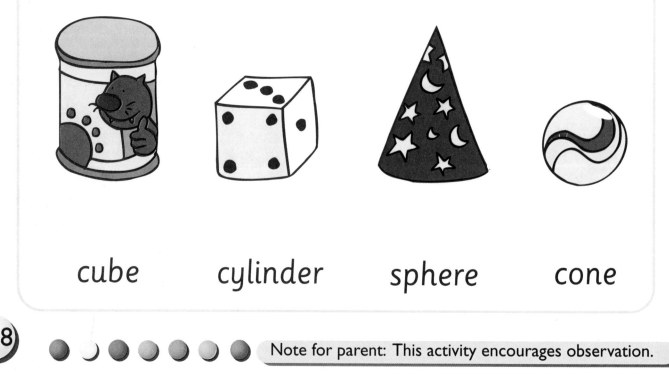

cube   cylinder   sphere   cone

Design a crazy outfit. Draw as many shapes as you can on the t-shirt, shorts, and shoes. Now add a pattern of shapes onto the skateboard.

Finish the pictures

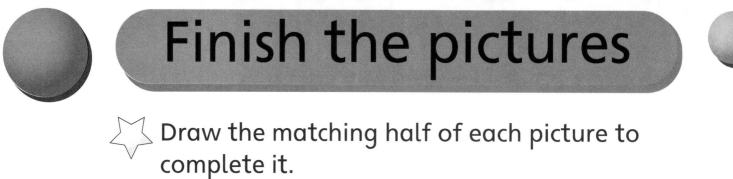

☆ Draw the matching half of each picture to complete it.

Note for parent: This activity encourages children to think about how to make things symmetrical.

In the house

⭐ Look at the picture and answer the questions. Write your answers on the lines. The first one has been done for you.

On which floor of the house is the cat? _first_

In which window? _____

On which floor of the house is the mouse? _____

In which window? _____

On which floor of the house is the girl? _____

In which window? _____

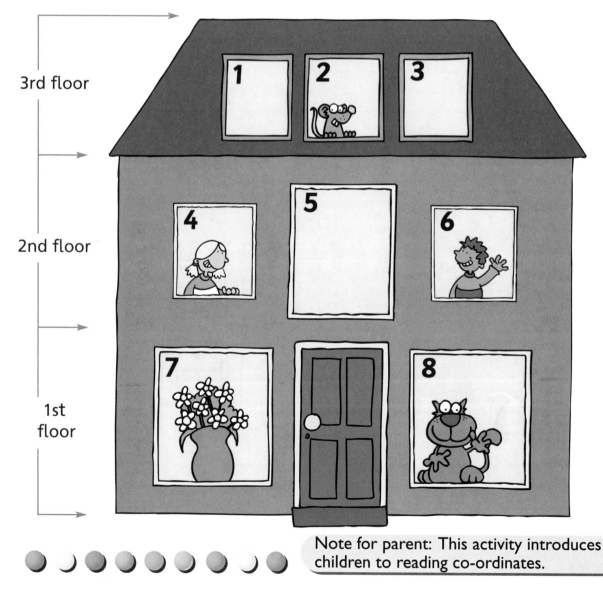

3rd floor

2nd floor

1st floor

Note for parent: This activity introduces children to reading co-ordinates.

Draw a picture of yourself on the first floor in window 8.
Draw a cat on the 2nd floor in window 4.
Draw a bat on the 3rd floor in window 3.
Color the picture.

Treasure hunt

The pirate is looking for treasure, but there are lots of things in his way. Follow the instructions to show him where the dangers are.

Column B, row 1 = cliffs. Color the square brown.

Column B, rows 2–4 = swamp. Color the squares orange.

Columns C + D, row 3 = jungle. Color the squares green.

Columns E + F, row 5 = river. Color the squares blue.

Columns D + E, row 2 = quicksand. Color the squares yellow.

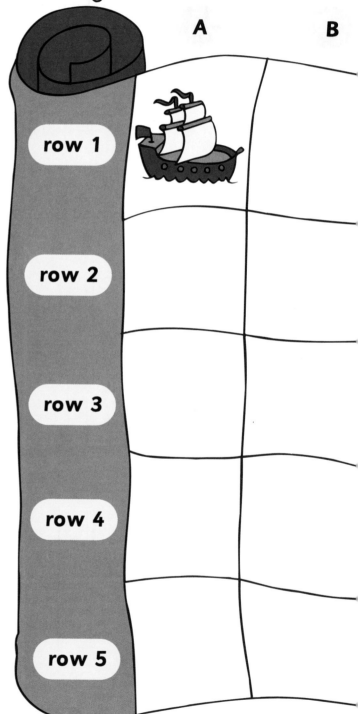

Note for parent: This activity provides further practice in reading co-ordinates.

Now draw a line from the pirate ship to the X, avoiding the dangers.

C   D   E   F

X

Tell the time

☆ Look at the clocks below. Draw a line to join each clock to the box with the same time.

9:00   3:00   6:00

Draw the hands

Read the times below the clocks. Draw the hands on each clock to say what time it is.

1:00

2:30

5:00

ten o'clock

eight o'clock

four-thirty

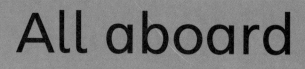

All aboard

☆ Look at the train timetable below. What time does each train leave? Draw the hands on the clock below each train to show the correct time.

> ### Train timetable
>
> **train 1 leaves at 7:00**
>
> **train 2 leaves at 5:15**
>
> **train 3 leaves at 6:30**
>
> **train 4 leaves at 5:30**
>
> **train 5 leaves at 6:45**

☆ Which train leaves first? Write your answer on the line.

_____

☆ Which train leaves last?

_____

train 1

train 2

train 3

train 4

train 5

219

⭐ Join the dots in each picture. Draw a line from each picture to the correct word to say which season it is.

Fall

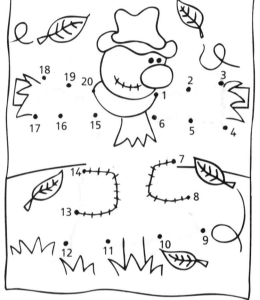

Summer

Spring

Winter

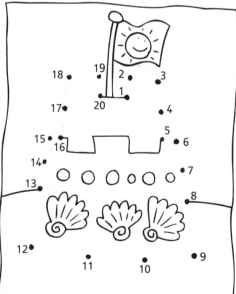

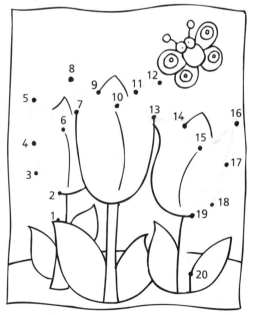

Note for parent: This activity provides practice in learning about seasons and the months of the year.

Look at these pages from a calendar.
Which months do you think they show?
Write the names of the months in the spaces.

1	2	3	4	5	6	7	8
9	10	11	12	13	14	15	16
17	18	19	20	21	22	23	24
	26	27	28	29	30	31	

1	2	3	4	5	6	7	8
9	10	11	12	13	14	15	16
17	18	19	20	21	22	23	24
25	26	27	28	29	30		

When is your birthday? Circle the date on
the calendar. Write the name of the month
in the space.

1	2	3	4	5	6	7	8
9	10	11	12	13	14	15	16
17	18	19	20	21	22	23	24
25	26	27	28	29	30	31	

Days of the week

Draw a line from each picture to the correct sentence. Draw a line under the day of the week in each sentence.

On **Wednesday**, Joe played a board game with his sister.

On **Friday**, Joe made a birthday card for his friend Sam.

Joe went swimming on **Monday**.

Joe went for a ride on his new bike on **Thursday**.

On **Tuesday**, Joe read a book before bedtime.

Joe went to town on the bus on **Sunday**.

On **Saturday**, Joe went to Sam's birthday party.

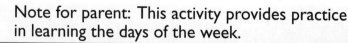

Note for parent: This activity provides practice in learning the days of the week.

My diary

Trace over the dotted letters in the diary. Write down something you did on each day last week. Write your answers on the lines.

Monday _____

Tuesday _____

Wednesday _____

Thursday _____

Friday _____

Saturday _____

Sunday _____

What did I do?

Look at these pictures. Complete the sentence under each picture. Use the words in the box to help you.

go   going   goes   went
will go
play   played
will play

Yesterday

I _____ to the fair.

Today

I _____ at the park.

Tomorrow

I _____ _____ fishing.

Note for parent: This activity provides practice in placing events in time.

Now draw and label your own pictures for yesterday, today, and tomorrow.

Yesterday

Today

_____

_____

Tomorrow

_____

_____

In a minute

★ This stopwatch counts 60 seconds, which is the same as 1 minute. You need a stopwatch or a watch with a second hand for this activity. Ask an adult to time you.

★ How many times in a minute can you …

touch your nose?

stand up and sit down?

Note for parent: This activity helps children to appreciate a limited time period.

clap?

take your hat on and off?

hop?

cross and uncross your legs?

Sums

Look at these sums. You can make them shorter by using the times sign x. Rewrite each adding sum as a times sum. The first one has been done for you.

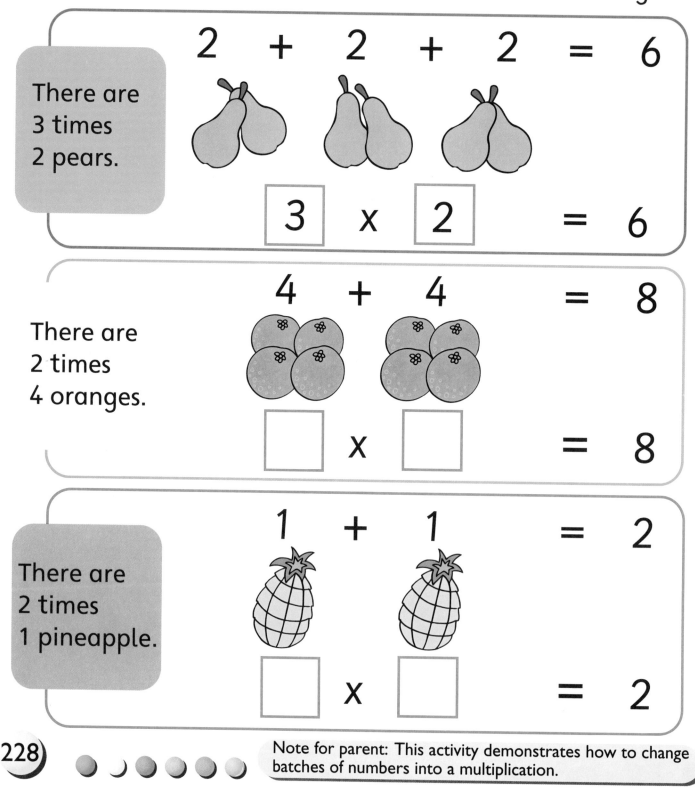

There are 3 times 2 pears.

2 + 2 + 2 = 6

3 x 2 = 6

There are 2 times 4 oranges.

4 + 4 = 8

☐ x ☐ = 8

There are 2 times 1 pineapple.

1 + 1 = 2

☐ x ☐ = 2

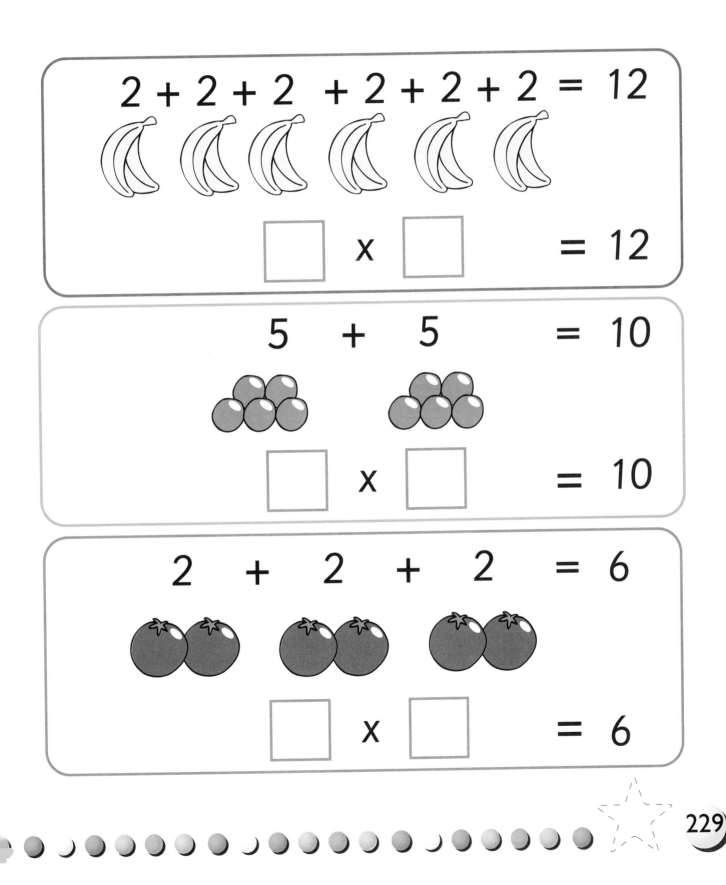

2 + 2 + 2 + 2 + 2 + 2 = 12

$\boxed{}$ x $\boxed{}$ = 12

5 + 5 = 10

$\boxed{}$ x $\boxed{}$ = 10

2 + 2 + 2 = 6

$\boxed{}$ x $\boxed{}$ = 6

Animal sums

Fill in the missing numbers to complete the sums.

3 x 1 cow = ☐ cows

☐ x 1 bee = 6 bees

3 x ☐ fish = 3 fish

Note for parent: This activity demonstrates how to add batches of numbers into a simplified multiplication.

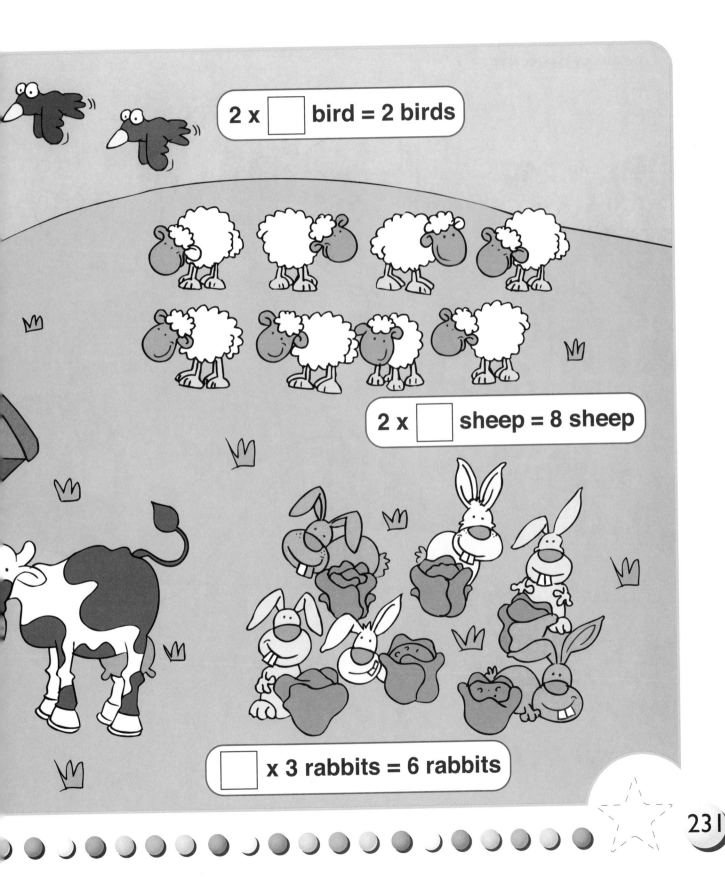

2 x ☐ bird = 2 birds

2 x ☐ sheep = 8 sheep

☐ x 3 rabbits = 6 rabbits

2 times table

⭐ Say the 2 times table aloud. Now fill out the missing numbers in the balloons to complete the sums.

☐ x 2 = 0

☐ x 2 = 6

5 x 2 = ☐

☐ x 2 = 8

1 x 2 = ☐

☐ x 2 = 4

Note for parent: This activity gives practice in learning the 2x table.

$0 \times 2 = 0$ $6 \times 2 = 12$
$1 \times 2 = 2$ $7 \times 2 = 14$
$2 \times 2 = 4$ $8 \times 2 = 16$
$3 \times 2 = 6$ $9 \times 2 = 18$
$4 \times 2 = 8$ $10 \times 2 = 20$
$5 \times 2 = 10$

$\boxed{} \times 2 = 16$

$\boxed{} \times 2 = 20$

$9 \times 2 = \boxed{}$

$6 \times 2 = \boxed{}$

$\boxed{} \times 2 = 14$

Double the bubbles

Fill out the missing numbers for the fish. The number in each big bubble is 2 times (2x) the number in the small bubble. The first one has been done for you.

Up in smoke

⭐ You have to times the numbers in the racing cars by 2 to work out the missing numbers. Write your answers in the smoke at the back of each car. The first one has been done for you.

Note for parent: This activity provides further practice in doubling numbers.

5 times table

⭐ Look at the laundry line. Say the times table aloud. Now fill out the missing numbers on the laundry baskets to complete the sums. The first one has been done for you.

$0 \times 5 = 0$

$1 \times 5 = 5$

$2 \times 5 = 10$

$3 \times 5 = 15$

$4 \times 5 = 20$

$\boxed{9} \times 5 = 45$

$4 \times 5 = \boxed{}$

$\boxed{} \times 5 = 5$

$\boxed{} \times 5 = 10$

Note for parent: This activity gives practice in learning the 5x table.

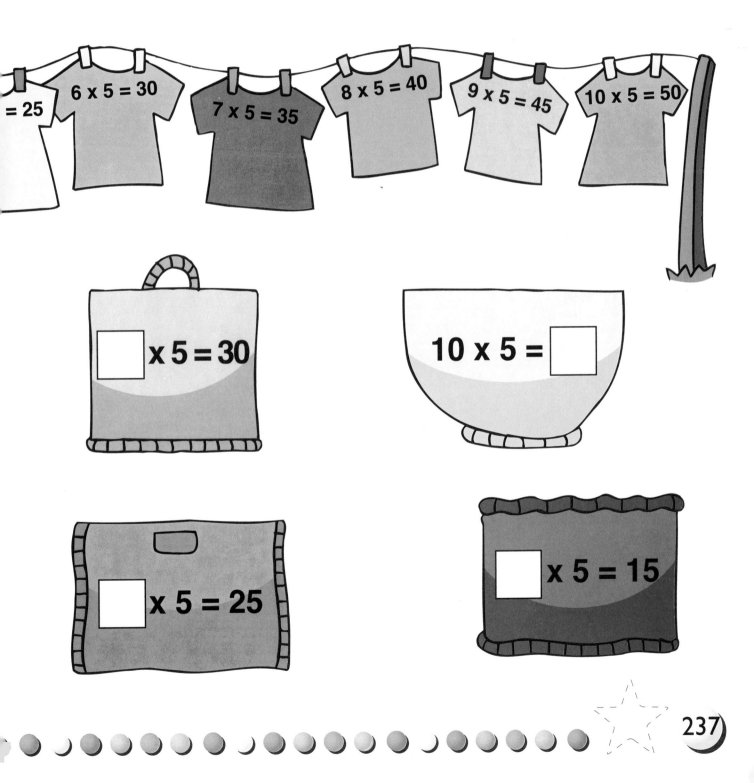

= 25

6 x 5 = 30

7 x 5 = 35

8 x 5 = 40

9 x 5 = 45

10 x 5 = 50

☐ x 5 = 30

10 x 5 = ☐

☐ x 5 = 25

☐ x 5 = 15

Fruity sums

Count the fruits in the boxes. Then work out the sums and write your answers in the empty boxes. The first one has been done for you.

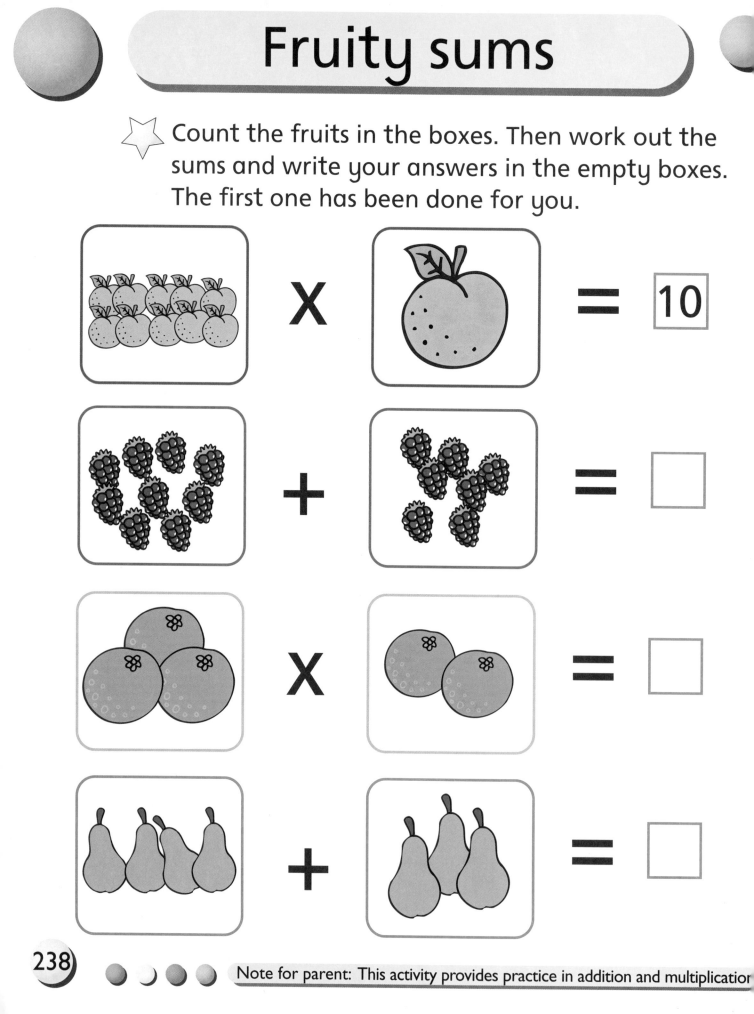

X = 10

+ =

X =

+ =

Note for parent: This activity provides practice in addition and multiplication

 **+**  **=**

 **X**  **=**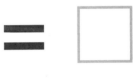

 **+**  **=**

239

10 times table

Say the 10 times table aloud. Now fill out the missing numbers to complete the sums. The first one has been done for you.

0 x 10 = 0

1 x 10 = 10

2 x 10 = 20

3 x 10 = 30

4 x 10 = 40

5 x 10 =

3 x 10 = ☐

2 x ☐ = 20

☐ x 10 = 70

☐ x 10 = 40

☐ x 10 = 90

Note for parent: This activity gives practice in learning the 10x table.

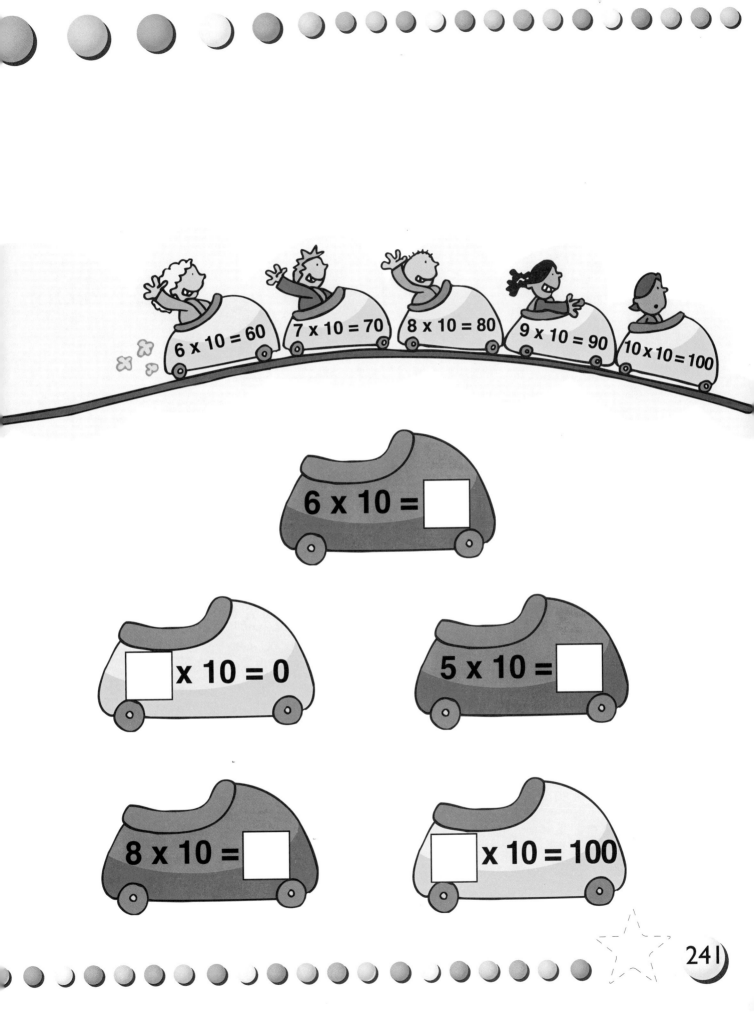

6 x 10 = 60

7 x 10 = 70

8 x 10 = 80

9 x 10 = 90

10 x 10 = 100

6 x 10 = □

□ x 10 = 0

5 x 10 = □

8 x 10 = □

□ x 10 = 100

⭐ Count the musical notes. Work out the answers to the sums. Write your answers in the empty boxes. The first one has been done for you.

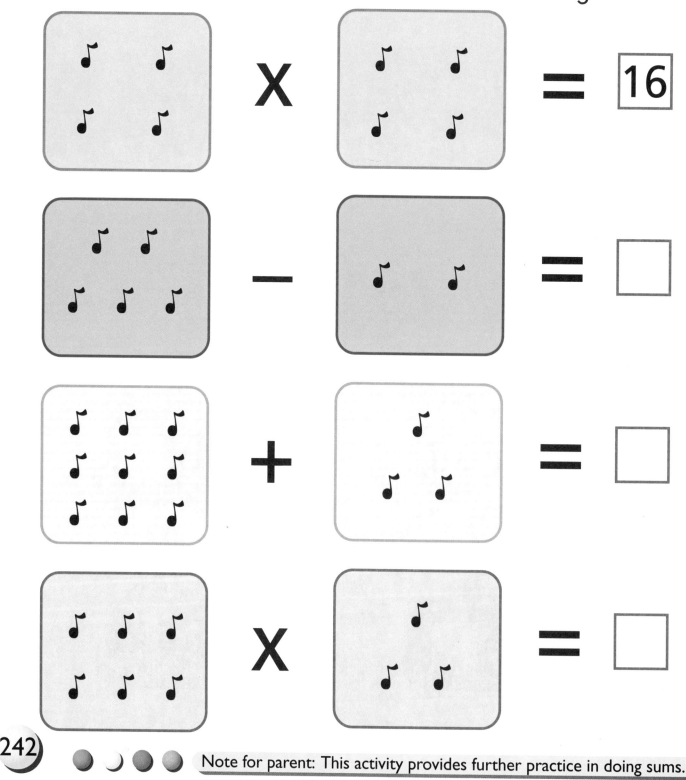

Note for parent: This activity provides further practice in doing sums.

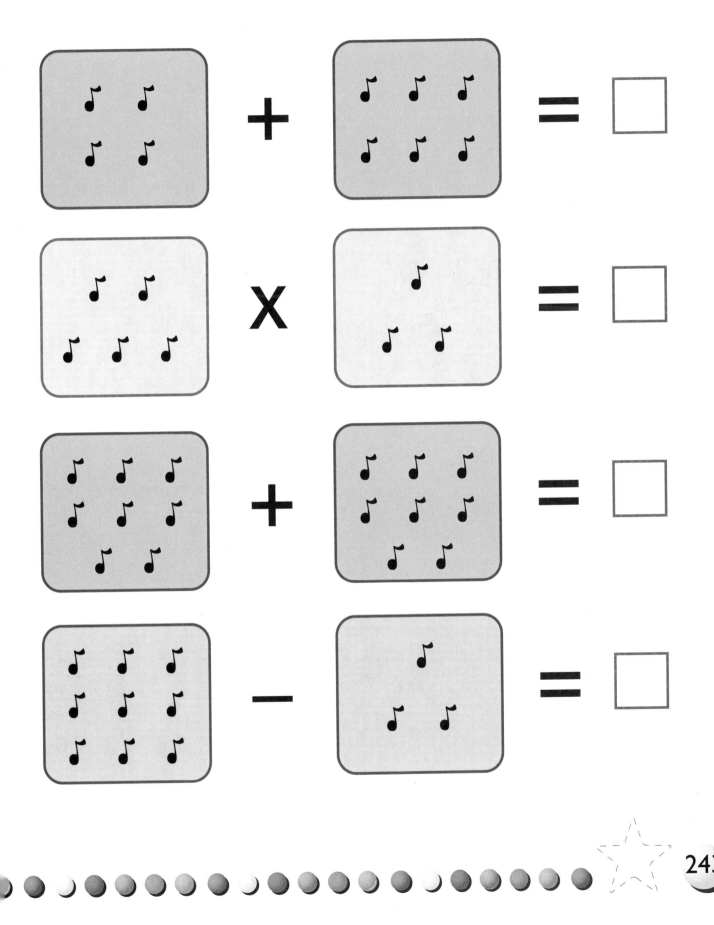

Sorting into sets

⭐ Ruby has 12 marbles. She has arranged them in 2 different ways. Can you help her to arrange the marbles in different ways? The first one has been done for you.

Draw 6 marbles in 2 ways:

Draw 10 marbles in 2 ways:

Draw 15 marbles in 2 ways:

Sharing out

There are 6 flowers and 12 bees. If you share the bees out equally, how many bees are there for each flower? Draw lines to join the bees to the flowers. Write the answer in the box.

Dinnertime sums

⭐ It's dinnertime for the animals. Work out how much food each animal will have. Write your answers in the boxes.

⭐ There are 6 dogs and 12 bones. How many bones will each dog have? ☐

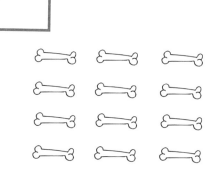

⭐ There are 3 rabbits and 12 carrots. How many carrots will each rabbit have? ☐

⭐ There are 3 birds and 9 worms. How many worms will each bird have? ☐

Note for parent: This activity provides further practice in sharing and division.

There are 5 cats and 10 fish. How many fish will each cat have? ☐

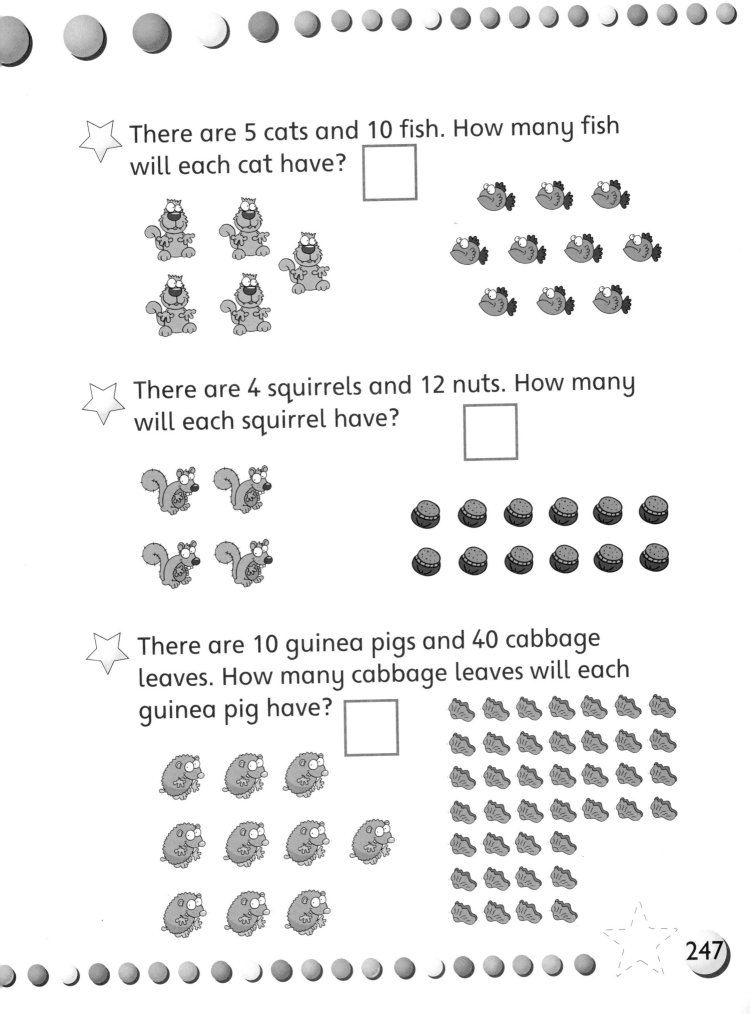

There are 4 squirrels and 12 nuts. How many will each squirrel have? ☐

There are 10 guinea pigs and 40 cabbage leaves. How many cabbage leaves will each guinea pig have? ☐

Trick or treat?

There are 3 trick-or-treaters. Each person gets an equal number of candies from each house. Count the candies and work out how many each person has. Write your answers in the boxes.

How many does each person get? ☐

How many does each person get? ☐

How many does
each person get?

How many does
each person get?

How many does
each person get?

How many does
each person get?

Equal shares

⭐ Look at the different foods. Divide each food into two equal shares to go in 2 lunch boxes. Write your answers in the boxes.

How many sandwiches in each lunch box? ☐

How many grapes in each lunch box? ☐

How many apples in each lunch box? ☐

How many juices in each lunch box? ☐

How many yogurts in each lunch box? ☐

Note for parent: This activity provides practice in halving sets of objects.

Dividing by 2

Look at the numbers in the small bubbles. Can you divide each one by 2? Write your answers in the big bubbles. The first one has been done for you.

Answers

Writing

Page 8

r	p	l	a	n	e	t	s
c	o	m	e	t	s	t	a
r	o	c	k	e	t	s	m
a	x	y	e	o	a	t	o
t	a	m	t	r	r	a	o
e	o	r	o	c	s	u	n
r	g	a	l	a	x	y	x
c	k	m	e	t	e	o	r

Page 10

a – A, b – B, c – C, d – D, e – E, f – F, g – G, h – H, i – I, j – J, k – K, l – L, m – M, n – N, o – O, p – P, q – Q, r – R, s – S, t – T, u – U, v – V, w – W, x – X, y – Y, z – Z.

Page 11

F – Fluffy, b – books, S – Sally, D – David, t – table, h – hat.

Page 12

horse – 4, dinosaurs – 2, trains – 10, insects – 5, snow – 10, queens – 9, alligators – 1.

Page 13

Alison, Billy, Chris, David, Eve, Fred.

Pages 14–15

King Alley, page 16; Bridge Road, page 5; Green Street, page 11; Acorn Way, page 2; Jumping Road, page 14; Farm Close, page 9; King Street, page 18; Frosty Way, page 10; Hill Road, page 12; Jumping Way, page 15.

Page 17

Sam sang silly songs. Bob blew big bubbles. Laura loves little ladybugs. Tim tripped two times. Wendy watches wild waves. Meg made more macaroni.

Pages 18–19

s – sky, seagulls, sun, sea, sand, sunhat, sunglasses, shirt, shorts, spade, sandcastle; p – pigtails, packets, pizza, peas, pasta, pineapples, pears, peaches;

f – fairy, flags, flowers, frog, fox, fish, feather; b – boat, belt, bed, box, bricks, ball, boots, book, balloon, bedside table.

Page 20

clown – brown, queen – green, bed – red, sink – pink, kite – white, hay – gray.

Page 21

Possible answers are: train–rain, dog–frog, mop–top, flag–bag, cake–rake, tree–bee.

Pages 22–23

blue – shoe, mat – hat, tall – ball, can – man, frown – clown.

Page 24

h	o	h	o	r	s	e	t
p	e	n	g	u	i	n	i
e	b	p	e	w	d	o	g
n	g	i	r	a	f	f	e
g	u	g	o	b	e	a	r
z	i	c	s	h	s	r	s
e	m	o	n	k	e	y	e
b	l	w	a	b	a	e	r
r	z	o	k	r	l	t	g
a	s	w	e	s	h	c	f

Page 25

1 down – cat; 2 down – mug; 3 down – pirate; 5 down – plate; 7 down – kite; 9 down – bed; 4 across – tiger; 6 across – cake; 8 across – table.

Pages 26–27

Page 31

Possible answers are: bed, pillow, curtains, lamp, bedside table, rug.

Page 32

Are you going swimming? That's great! It's my birthday! What time is it? I am six years old.

Page 35

She is hiding under the bed.

Page 36

1. 4 tablespoons of cream;
2. 2 bars of chocolate;
3. decorations; 4. when the chocolate melts; 5. Yes.

Page 37

Page 40

Possible answers are: house, cat, ladder, dog, fire truck.

Page 41

1. mug, 2. teddy bear, 3. dog, 4. door, 5. ball.

Page 42

picture – sunny, bright; vase – yellow, fresh; witch – ugly, old; car – shiny, red.

Page 43

Kate's hair is brown. Her dress is pink. She is wearing a bow in her hair. Possible adjectives are: pretty, young. Joe's hair is curly. His shirt is striped. He is holding a skateboard. Possible adjectives are: tall, sporty.

Pages 46–47

Pirate: I'm a pirate who looks for treasure.
Doctor: I will make you better when you are ill.
Vampire: I'm a scary vampire.
Wizard: I can do magic tricks.
Clown: I hope my jokes make you laugh.

Page 50

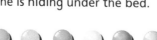

Page 54
beware – ducks crossing the field.

Page 55
The third floor of the art gallery.

Page 65
lion, goat, kangaroo, turtle, zebra, rhinoceros.

Page 66
roller-skates, van, car, boat, helicopter.

Page 67
ant, spider, dragonfly, butterfly, fly, caterpillar.

Pages 68–69
tractor, hay, horse, sheep, field, cat, pig, cow, hen, chick.

Page 70
balloon, gift, cake, card, banner.

Page 71
window, lamp, rug, bed.

Page 72
trees, house, car, road, park, swing.

Pages 74–75
The fat cat sat on the mat. The frog hopped on top of the mop. The wicked witch flew west to fetch a vest. The furry mouse ran around the house. The pink kite flies high in the sky.

Pages 76–77

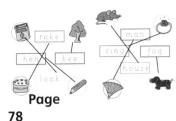

Page 78
dish – fish, top – mop, jug – mug, car – jar, jam – ham.

Page 79
hat – cat, wall – ball, mug – rug, stamp – lamp, boat – coat.

Page 80
sp – spoon, spin, spot; sk – skin, skid, skip.

Page 81
cl – club, clap, clear, cling, clue; st – stair, stem, step.

Page 82

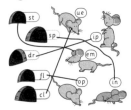

Page 83
In the picture are 3 mice and a piece of cheese.

Page 84

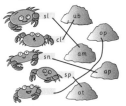

Page 85
In the picture are a crab, some fish, and other creatures in an underwater scene.

Page 86
ss – hiss, miss, kiss, mess, fuss, less; ll – shell, ball, doll, pull, small, well.

Page 87
nk – wink, drink, pink, blink, sink; ck – pick, tick, sack, lock, rock, clock, sock.

Page 88

Page 89
In the picture is a skateboarder.

Page 90

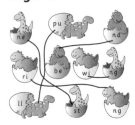

Page 91
a dinosaur

Page 92

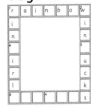

Page 93
1 across – snowman; 3 across – letter; 2 down – door; 4 down – cake; 5 down – picture.

Pages 94–95
oa – goal, road, toad, float; ow – blow, slow, throw, grow.

Pages 96–97
oo – moon, spoon, soon, roof; ew – flew, blew, grew, new; ue – glue, blue, true, clue.

Pages 98–99
y – sky, my, fly, cry; ie – lie, pie.

Pages 100–101
1 – one; 2 – two; 3 – three; 4 – four; 5 – five; 6 – six; 7 – seven; 8 – eight; 9 – nine; 10 – ten.

Pages 102–103
11 – eleven; 12 – twelve; 13 – thirteen; 14 – fourteen; 15 – fifteen; 16 – sixteen; 17 – seventeen; 18 – eighteen; 19 – nineteen; 20 – twenty.

Page 104
1 – potatoes; 2 – carrots; 3 – onions; 4 – broccoli; 5 – tomatoes; 6 – peas.

Page 105
chocolate, flour, milk, sugar, eggs.

Page 106
shorts, pajamas, jeans, dress, shirt, socks.

Page 107
snake skin, bats' wings, spiders' legs, toad stools.

Page 108

snake, monkey, seal, giraffe

Page 110

star, moon, rocket, alien, planet.

Page 111

window, light, door, wheel

Page 112

spoon, juice, toast, cereal

Page 113

hair, eye, ear, nose, mouth

Page 114

Page 122

Page 123

1 across – castle; 3 across – milk;
2 down – wizard; 5 down – tree;
4 down – eggs.

Pages 124–125

✔ – donkey, sun, blue, mouse, shirt,
deer, bear, flower.

Pages 126–127

wet paint, STOP, Beware, Toys and
Games, Road closed, School, Ice
cream, Pizza.

Reading

Page 129

r – rocket, robot; t – train,
teddy bear; d – drum, dinosaur;
the washing machine and the cook
do not belong. There are other
possible answers.

Pages 130–131

1. Butterflies <u>have</u> two wings.
2. The children <u>play</u> in the park.
3. The cat <u>meows</u> at the dog.
4. Dad <u>washes</u> the car.
5. The mailman <u>rings</u> the doorbell.
6. I have <u>cereal</u> for breakfast.
7. The mouse <u>eats</u> the cheese.
8. There are <u>stars</u> in the sky.
9. Penguins <u>swim</u> in the water.
10. The train is <u>going</u> to town.
11. I wear <u>slippers</u> on my feet.

Page 132

people: girl, doctor; things: mug,
t-shirt; animals: cat, rabbit.

Pages 134–135

I cook food. I build houses. I drive
the bus. I bake bread. I teach
children. I check teeth. I grow
vegetables.

Page 136

The verbs are: climbs, jumps, hops,
paddles, wags.

Page 137

kicking, sliding, flying, swinging,
digging.

Pages 138–139

The verbs are: eats, rides, plays,
makes, watches, puts, reads.

Page 140

My name <u>is</u> Sarah. I <u>am</u> Sarah's
friend, Ben. Sarah and Ben <u>are</u>
going to the library.

Page 141

1. The children <u>are</u> at the
swimming pool. 2. The girl <u>is</u>
standing by the pool. 3. The boys
<u>are</u> swimming. 4. The instructor <u>is</u>
blowing a whistle.

Page 142

Page 143

1. yes, 2. yes, 3. yes, 4. no.

Page 144

ring – shiny; mug – hard; chair –
comfortable; ice – cold; shoe – old.

Page 146

elephant – big; rabbit – fluffy;
tortoise – slow; mouse – little;
zebra – stripy.

Page 148

There are 7 differences.

Page 150

b. The clown is making the
children happy. c. The little boy is
eating ice cream. a. The cat is
watching two fish.

Page 156

Page 160

newspaper – c; magazine – a;
comic – b.

Page 161
animals – 2; science – 3; mystery – 1.

Page 162

Page 163

Page 164
1. Bag 3; 2. Bag 2 and Bag 3;
3. Bag 1; 4. Bags 1 and 3; 5. Bag 2.

Pages 166–167
1. Mary; 2. Sam; 3. Sam; 4. Mary.
1. They are going for a swim at
2:15. 2. At 9:00 they are going to
the museum. 3. Just before lunch
they are walking along the river.

Page 168

Page 169
1. A carnival. 2. 10:00 pm. 3. The
tickets are free. 4.Yes.

Page 171
1. true; 2. false; 3. false; 4. true;
5. false.

Page 172
1. The mouse sees a piece of
cheese. 2. The cat chases the
mouse. 3. The dog chases the cat.
4. The mouse eats the cheese.

Page 173
1. There is a full plate of cookies.
2. Now there are only three. 3.
Who is eating the cookies? 4. A
monster has eaten all the cookies!

Page 174
The wizard looks in his book for a
special brew. 2. He mixes the
ingredients. 3. Then he casts the
spell. 4. "Perfect brew," he says.

Page 175
1. A little boy draws a picture for
his Grandma. 2. He puts the
picture in an envelope. 3. Then he
mails it. 4. The mailman collects it
from the mail box. 5. Another
postman delivers it. 6. Grandma
loves her drawing!

Page 176

Page 177

Page 179
Can you feed the ducks? No. Can
you ride a bicycle? No. Can you
swim in the pond? No. Can you put
garbage in the trash can bin? Yes.

Page 180

Page 182
Route c.

Page 183
7 eyes of frog – ✗;
6 bats' wings – ✗; swamp gas – ✔;
4 sets of false teeth – ✗;
green slime – ✔.

Page 185

Page 187
1. false; 2. false; 3. true; 4. true.

Page 189
1. The roller-coaster is going up.
2 The girl's ice cream is on the
ground. 3. The dog wants to eat
the girl's ice cream. 4. There are 5
people on the roller-coaster.
5. The prize for the ball game is a
teddy bear. 6. The juggler is
juggling 5 balls.

Page 190
1. Tuesday; 2. Saturday; 3.
Monday; 4. Saturday and Sunday;
5. Thursday.

Page 191
1 – d; 2 – a; 3 – b; 4 – c.

Math

Page 193
7, 15, 15, 20, 16, 9, 3, 14, 10.

Page 194
1, 3, 5, 10, 15.

Page 195
snake: 13 inch, pencil: 11 inch;
kite: 12 inch. The present is 4 inch
tall and 6 inch wide.

Page 198
A triangle has 3 sides; a pentagon
has 5 sides; a hexagon has 6 sides;
an octagon has 8 sides; a square
has 4 sides; a rectangle has 4 sides.

Page 199
All 4 sides of a square are the
same length. The opposite sides of
a rectangle are the same length.
A circle is round. An oval is egg-
shaped.

Page 203
cylinder, cube, sphere, prism.

Page 204

Page 205

Page 206

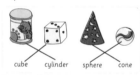

Page 207

Page 208

top row: △ bottom row: ⬠

cube   cylinder   sphere   cone

Page 212

The cat is on the first floor, in window 8. The mouse is on the 3rd floor, in window 2. The girl is on the 2nd floor, in window 4.

Pages 214–215

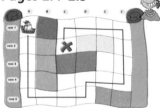

Page 216

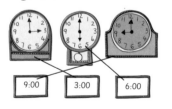

9:00   3:00   6:00

Page 217

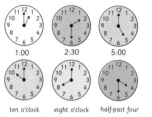

1:00   2:30   5:00

ten o'clock   eight o'clock   half-past four

Page 218

Train 2 leaves first. Train 1 leaves last.

Page 219

7:00   5:15   6:30

5:30   6:45

Page 220

Fall   Summer
Spring   Winter

Page 221

December and October.

Page 222

On **Wednesday**, Joe played a board game with his sister.
On **Friday**, Joe made a birthday card for his friend Sam.
Joe went swimming on **Monday**.
Joe went for a ride on his new bike on **Thursday**.
On **Tuesday**, Joe read a book before bedtime.
Joe went to town on the bus on **Sunday**.
On **Saturday**, Joe went to Sam's birthday party.

Page 224

Yesterday I went to the fair. Today I play at the park. Tomorrow I will go fishing.

Pages 228–229

2 x 4 = 8; 2 x 1 = 2; 6 x 2 = 12; 2 x 5 = 10; 3 x 2 = 6.

Pages 230–231

3 x 1 cow = 3 cows; 6 x 1 bee = 6 bees; 3 x 1 fish = 3 fish; 2 x 1 bird = 2 birds; 2 x 4 sheep = 8 sheep;

2 x 3 rabbits = 6 rabbits.

Pages 232–233

left clown: 0 x 2 = 0; 3 x 2 = 6; 5 x 2 = 10; 4 x 2 = 8; 1 x 2 = 2; 2 x 2 = 4; right clown: 8 x 2 = 16; 10 x 2 = 20; 9 x 2 = 18; 6 x 2 = 12; 7 x 2 = 14.

Page 234

2 x 2 = 4; 4 x 2 = 8; 1 x 2 = 2; 3 x 2 = 6; 8 x 2 = 16; 5 x 2 = 10.

Page 235

9 x 2 = 18; 5 x 2 = 10; 8 x 2 = 16; 4 x 2 = 8; 6 x 2 = 12; 2 x 2 = 4; 4 x 2 = 8; 1 x 2 = 2; 11 x 2 = 22.

Pages 236–237

4 x 5 = 20; 1 x 5 = 5; 2 x 5 = 10; 6 x 5 = 30; 10 x 5 = 50; 5 x 5 = 25; 3 x 5 = 15.

Pages 238–239

9 + 7 = 16; 3 x 2 = 6; 4 + 3 = 7; 9 + 8 = 17; 4 x 2 = 8; 6 + 7 = 13; 10 x 2 = 20.

Pages 240–241

2 x 10 = 20; 7 x 10 = 70; 4 x 10 = 40; 9 x 10 = 90; 6 x 10 = 60; 0 x 10 = 0; 5 x 10 = 50; 8 x 10 = 80; 10 x 10 = 100.

Pages 242–243

5 – 2 = 3; 9 + 3 = 12; 6 x 3 = 18; 4 + 6 = 10; 5 x 3 = 15; 8 + 8 = 16; 9 – 3 = 6.

Page 245

The answer is 2.

Page 246–247

2 bones; 4 carrots; 3 worms; 2 fish; 3 nuts; 4 cabbage leaves.

Pages 248–249

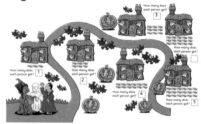

Page 250

2 sandwiches; 5 grapes; 1 apple; 1 juice; 1 yogurt.

Page 251

18 ÷ 2 = 9; 20 ÷ 2 = 10; 8 ÷ 2 = 4; 6 ÷ 2 = 3; 4 ÷ 2 = 2.